CHRISTIAN HULL

Leave Me ALONE

A MEMOIR OF ME, MYSELF & Trish

ALLEN&UNWIN
SYDNEY · MELBOURNE · AUCKLAND · LONDON

First published in 2021

Copyright © Christian Hull 2021

Allen & Unwin
83 Alexander Street
Crows Nest NSW 2065
Australia
Phone: (61 2) 8425 0100
Email: info@allenandunwin.com
Web: www.allenandunwin.com

 A catalogue record for this book is available from the National Library of Australia

ISBN 978 1 76087 653 1

Cover photography by Locky V Creative Photography © 2020, www.lockyv.com
Set in 10.6/19.2 pt Caecilia LT Std by Bookhouse, Sydney
Printed and bound in Australia by Griffin Press, part of Ovato

10 9 8 7 6 5 4 3 2

The paper in this book is FSC® certified. FSC® promotes environmentally responsible, socially beneficial and economically viable management of the world's forests.

For Mum and Dad

[Please put this in large font size so they can read it]

CONTENTS

PREFACE

If you know who I am, you are in a small minority of people and I love you. I really, really do. If you don't know who I am, then let me explain.

VITAL STATISTICS

DOB: 6 January 1987.

Height: Short.

Weight: Heavy.

Sex: All of it. Always trying to get it. Need it now. Thanks. That was average. Please leave.

Star sign: Grindr.

Religion: Caramilk.

VITAL NON-STATISTICS

1. I hate being social.
2. I love living alone.
3. I like being alone.
4. I have no pets.
5. I have no responsibilities.
6. (Apart from my indoor plants.)
7. I have never been in a relationship.
8. I never want to be in a relationship.
9. I lost my virginity at age twenty-three.
10. My phone data plan is huge because . . . porn.
11. I have lots of knick-knacks.
12. My two-bedroom apartment is full of cool stuff.
13. I love herbal tea.
14. I hate reading (except for my own book, of course).
15. I have a successful (that's arrogant) YouTube channel and Facebook page.
16. I love putting on wigs and making funny videos.
17. I have a small group of friends.
18. I love my life.

When people meet me, their first impression is that I am loud and confident—and I am. However, people often mistake loudness and confidence for fun. I am not fun. I am, in fact, super boring.

People assume that because my thing is making videos for strangers on the internet that I am a people person, one hundred per cent extraverted and the life of the party. People often think the Christian—or the Trish—they see in my videos is someone whose friend they'd want to be.

If you are one of those people, I am sorry to inform you that I do not want to be your friend. I have enough friends—at last count, five really good ones—and between them and my family, that's more than enough for me.*

The thing is, despite my choice of career, I am the last thing from a people person. I am a ME person. ME ME ME! And only me. Wonderful and weird me! And you know what? I am totally okay with that. The truth is, I am a total introvert. I love my own company and I can entertain myself for hours—or days or weeks—without ever feeling lonely or bored.

During my extensive and closely guarded 'me time', what I love to do most is create things: sculptures using wire, resin jewellery, even (admittedly, somewhat wonky-looking) concrete pots for my plants! I also love rearranging my apartment, making hand-made cards and scrolling through Grindr for hours and hours and hours to the point where I have lost track of what day it even is.

*Please note, I am happy to be swarmed by loving fans and do selfies and stuff, just not friendship. A selfie takes five seconds whereas some friendships can annoyingly last a lifetime.

But, most of all, what I love is making funny little videos which I then send out to the world via the modern-day Holy Trinity: YouTube, Facebook and Instagram.

And these days, my funny little videos are even my full-time job. How freaking lucky am I!

But it hasn't always been that way—Lady Luck and I are relatively new acquaintances, and to be honest I still don't really know whether I fully trust the bitch.

My first stroke of AMAZING LUCK, I should say upfront, was being born to parents like my mum and dad. I think it was pretty clear pretty early on that young Christian Munro Hull was not going to be like all the other boys. And not just because I am so gay that I literally came through my mother's birth canal doing jazz hands, but because I have always been just a little bit . . . extra!

If all the world's a stage and if life is a cabaret (old chum), then I have always always always always wanted to be the star of that show. And even though it took the rest of the world three decades to get the fucking memo, my family knew that pretty much from day one. And they have always been my biggest supporters and greatest fans—hey, don't knock a captive audience, sometimes they've all you've got!

Like I said, though, the rest of the world took a little bit longer to come to its senses about me. High school was terrible and my career in radio has had more ups and downs than a quickie blow job in a dark alley. Sometimes, it was hard to keep

believing in myself and accept that I am not everybody's—
and by 'everybody', I mostly mean management's—cup of tea.

I have had times where I have just had to withdraw from
the world because I couldn't find a place for myself in it. I have
had times where I have doubted myself and whether I was
ever going to make it and get the fuck out of retail. (Thank
god, and I *cannot* say this strongly enough, THANK GOD I did.)

But you know what? I got to a point where I just said:
fuck it.

Myself is the only person I know how to be, and the only
person I am good at being. There comes a time where you just
have to embrace what you've got—including the love handles
and man boobs—and just force the world to accept you as you
are and get it to work for you and not the other way around.
And if people don't like it? Well, just wave them on.

So, this book is how I do me. (Haha! I said 'do me'—that's
a daily ritual!)

How I came to be me, the (maybe one or two) things I love,
the (about 4356) things I hate, the (many many) things (guys)
I have done and the things I would never do again. How I have
managed to still be myself in a world that hasn't always understood me. How I have done life on my terms and why I am
not the least bit apologetic for it.

After all, who wants to fit the fucking mould? The mould
is boring, the mould is old hat, the mould needs a goddamn
makeover. I say, don't just break the mould, smash it into a

million pieces and then refashion it into an amazing pendant that tells people to fuck off.

At the ripe old age of thirty-three, that's what I have figured out. And while there are still many, many things that I have not figured out (what the blue, then orange and now flashing red light on my car's dashboard means), I think figuring out that life is short and you may as well just be yourself is the most important—and sometimes the hardest—thing to learn.

So, put on a pair of trackies, pull the blinds closed, put your phone on silent, grab a KitKat Gold (or five) and settle in.

Welcome to the world of Christian Hull.

Sorry, not sorry!

Part One

MY PEOPLE

1

LOVE, A STEAMY NOVEL AND TRIPLE TROUBLE

My family are my world. Actual world.

I currently live and work in Brisbane and before that I lived in Melbourne for six years. My whole family lives in Sydney, which I pretend I'm okay with but, when it comes down to it, I hate it. For one thing, it means I mostly have to watch my nieces grow up via Facebook. But when I do visit, they are there yelling and screaming at me to watch them jump on the trampoline or watch them riding their scooters or watch them do the most boring things of all time. It's super cute and I love it, but I also get bored of it quickly—like, how many times do I have to watch you jump in the air? I miss hanging out with them on a whim.

I only have myself to blame for this. I could easily pack up shop and return home and work from there and be near them.

them. I often feel really bad that I am not there with Mum and Dad—they have done so much for me and I feel like I have just abandoned them. Like their lives now lack purpose and meaning because I cannot be their everyday focus. I mean, I am totally overreacting but that's just how I feel. Guilty.

I have older parents: Dad was thirty-nine when I was born and Mum was thirty-three. Dad worked for Qantas as a Flight Service Director, and Mum was a fashion designer who worked for a few big labels. Just to make it clear: Dad worked as a hostie and Mum worked in fashion—two of the biggest gay industries. They were destined to have a gay son. Both my parents were very smart with their finances and with wise investments and my dad's carpentry skills, they were able to buy and renovate an amazing house in Denistone for the big family they were unknowingly going to have. They had virtually paid off their mortgage by the time my brothers came along.

Mum (aka Karen aka Supreme Leader) and Dad (aka John aka 'yes darl') are the definition of chalk and cheese. You could not get two people who are more different. Mum is a lover of art and I get the sense she was a total hippie back in the day. Dad is a hater of art and was in the CMF—the civilian army. Literally, so opposite.

But when I look at photos of the two of them from centuries ago, back when the telephone was just being invented and I thought colour was yet to be discovered, I can see why they may have been drawn to each other. They were both super hot! Mum was a babe and Dad was such a dude.

So their similarities included having strong relationships with their families and both being attractive. It's not a long list but it is the inspiration behind my Grindr bio.

The way my parents met is one of the funniest stories. I only recently found out about it because I was asked to include it in the book. I phoned up Dad to ask him about their first meeting, and he then put me on speaker and brought Mum into the conversation. I could not stop laughing throughout the entire phone call at their bickering about how it happened. Here is what I was told.

Dad was working on a Qantas flight flying from Europe to Sydney. He noticed a lovely-looking lady in section 'E' as he recalls. We are talking like nine decades ago when planes had sections. Mum was in her late twenties and Dad was in his early thirties. He worked up the nerve to strike up a little bit of a conversation with her.

Dad had noticed that Mum was reading a book. Nothing out of the ordinary, just a boring novel. Except Mum had concealed another book behind this boring novel. She was reading, as she calls it, a very 'steamy book'. But she didn't want the other passengers to judge her, so she hid it. Dad had noticed this.

He walked up to her and said hello and asked if there was anything she needed. Mum said she thought he was very handsome so happily decided to chat to him. When Dad then asked her what she was reading, she showed him the cover of the boring novel to which he said, 'What about the book behind that one?'

At this point of Mum and Dad's recount, I was dying with laughter. I only know my mum as such a goody-two-shoes, so this was revelatory—and hysterical—to me. Mum was reading a sexy novel when she first met Dad!

Dad got Mum's number and later called her and they went on their first date. The details of this first date differ greatly between them. Mum claims another friend, Daryl, was also there but Dad says they hadn't met Daryl yet at that point. Mum recalls that they went to an art gallery, but Dad says he doesn't remember that. At this point in the phone call, I just decided to leave them to argue it out. But I think their first date was a double date with Mum's sister Helen and my now Uncle David.

It's always fun going through old photos of Mum and Dad. Their wedding was in 1980 and seemed fairly low-key—it was held at Mum's parents' house and the bride and groom both looked so stunning! Mum had shorter hair and what I would describe as an elegantly simple wedding dress—not too flashy. She isn't a flashy person—I can't imagine her in anything over the top. She looked simply beautiful.

I came along in 1987 and turned their world upside-down—I was (am) the best thing that ever happened to them! I was a January baby—the sixth, to be exact. Please send gifts! I was a needy child (gee, what a shock) and arrived a few days before I was due. And, my god, was I an ugly baby! You know how parents can't see the ugliness in their children? Well, my parents were just as blind as the next set of doting parents. They still say I was the most beautiful child they had ever seen, but when you see the pics—I was an alien, so gross. SO UGLY!

Love truly is blind—and thank *god* for me that it is. Mum and Dad took me home, loved me with all their hearts and devoted themselves to caring for me.

But it wasn't just me for too long. I think they eventually realised what a dud I was and after almost five glorious years in my role of Little Prince, the Centre Of All Attention, the Most Important Boy In All The World, I was about to be dealt a severe blow.

In 1991, my parents had triplet boys. Yes, triplets. One. Two. Three. They are Nicholas, Timothy and Adrian—or, as Mum calls them, Nicky, Timmy and Ady. Wow, Mum! How on earth did you come up with such creative nicknames? I personally would have gone for Sleepy, Dopey and Dull—and that's just for Adrian. Together as brothers, we are 'CANT': Christian, Adrian, Nick and Tim. This was what my grandfather George used to call us. If only Adrian had been named Ulysses, then we could have been called something respectable.

What I will say right off the bat is that Mum and Dad are outstanding parents—they have raised three amazing children and Nick.

Though, like most little shits, at the time I didn't realise how good we had it. Mum gave up everything to have us and still gives up most of her life to this day to do things for us—for example, just the other day, she spent hours going to different op shops to get me hoodies for my little side business.

And Dad—well, he worked himself to the bone to provide for us. When he wasn't working, he was building us a cubby-house or renovating a new room for us to play in. Even at age seventy, he still can't help himself. When my brother Tim bought a place, Dad was over there in a flash—fixing and renovating it. Then Adrian bought a place and Dad was over there too, renovating it. It's like, slow the fuck down, Dad! When I buy a place, I need you to be fit and healthy to renovate it too!

I remember that the birth of my younger brothers seemed scary for my mum and dad and I never knew why. Years later, I found out that Mum had actually carried twin boys, Matthew and Anthony, before me and she gave birth to them but moments after they were born, they slipped away into the night. The reason why my parents were so scared throughout the pregnancy with the triplets was because of that. If Mum couldn't carry twins, how would she go with triplets?

There are some things you find out about your parents later in life that just make you look at them with absolute awe. This must have been such a scary and terrifying thing for them to go through and I was so young and had absolutely no idea. I wish I hadn't been such a little shit and that I somehow could have made the nine months Mum was pregnant a little easier for her and for Dad. I say that now, but the truth is that the screaming, crying and complaining I went on with as an inconsiderate toddler has actually carried through to my thirties—why would I break a trend that seems to be working for me?

If I am honest, in some awful selfish way, I am thankful that things happened the way they did. In all likelihood, Mum and Dad would not have had me had Matthew and Anthony survived. In a really twisted way, they gave me my life. We have visited my older brothers' graves a few times and I often wonder what it would be like if Matthew and Anthony were alive. I'm not religious, but I like to think they are watching out for us.

So, back to the triplets. The day came when Mum went into labour and I don't actually remember much of it. I do remember staying with our neighbour, Jan, for a few nights. Being only four, I just honestly had no idea what was happening, but they dangled food, a heated pool and lots of attention in front of me and I instantly forgot all about my family and what was going on. Jan and her kids made the next few days the best.

But, alas, I was to never return home and be the centre of attention. Life was about to change. Robert Frost talks about coming to a fork in the road—for me one path led to eternal happiness, all the attention again, and the other led to a life of misery. I picked the one that led to eternal happiness. PLOT TWIST! You thought I was going to say misery but my life has been so awesome since my brothers arrived.

It turns out the triplets were born super prematurely—Nick and Tim were identical and Adrian was the third. It was touch-and-go for my brother Adrian as there were some complications and issues with his health, but thankfully he was in a good hospital and would ultimately be okay.

Eventually came the day I was to meet them. It was like an episode from *The X-Files*. I had to put on a mask and gown and then I was taken in, to watch them lying there, looking a lot like aliens, in a humidicrib. Phrases like 'Aren't they adorable!' and 'So cute!' are usually associated with meeting newborn babies. Not with these guys! Instead, the phrases going through my head were more along the lines of 'Ew' and 'Get that thing away from me'. They were super gross-looking and they had sticky tape and tubes all over them. But flash forward twenty-nine years and—scandalously and completely unfairly—they are the ones who got all the good-looking genes and I'm the one who looks like a moon-shaped alien from the planet Cheese.

But back on that first day, I honestly had no idea who they were or what I was doing there. It was like some weird family outing to the zoo, but these baby animals were the kind you poked with a stick and threw carrots at, then ran away.

Due to how premature the boys were, Mum and Dad were in the hospital around the clock for weeks. My extended family were amazing and super supportive to Mum and Dad, and I remember staying with my aunt Helen, Mum's older sister.

After a few weeks of hell for Mum and Dad, it was finally home time for Nick and Tim. Sadly, Adrian had to spend a little more time in hospital. I do remember being confused as to why Mum and Dad kept saying I had three brothers. As a four-year-old, I slightly understood a mother giving birth to one child, but my brain couldn't grasp three. I thought it was like a baby buffet—some sort of try-before-you-buy deal. And I remember picking one and wondering if Mum and Dad would choose the same one I had picked. To this day, I wonder if this experience has led to my addiction to the buffet-style meal—instead of taking one, I take three.

I have one vivid memory of being upstairs with Mum and Dad, who were holding Nick and Tim. Mum was explaining to me why Adrian wasn't with us and what was wrong with him. There were tears from Mum and that's the moment I realised that something was wrong and also that I had three brothers, not just one, so there were a lot of tears from me too. 'But I just want none of them,' I proclaimed, making the situation all about me, as usual.

All the drama with Adrian settled down eventually and he was finally allowed home. We had to take special care of him and he required a little extra attention than Nick and Tim (how the tables have turned).

As much as I pretended that I hated suddenly having three brothers, I actually thought it was the coolest thing ever, mainly because most people only got one, so I thought I was getting a better deal than everyone else, which is really the only thing I ever wanted. That excitement never left and to this day I am still so grateful that I have three of the most amazing brothers.

Nick and Tim being identical makes them so goddamn competitive with each other. They are so unbelievably the same, but also so different. Heaps of people still can't tell them apart, which always boggles my mind because to me they do not look identical at all, they look quite different.

Tim can speak underwater with a mouth full of cement. Growing up, he never stopped to take a breath—a quality Mum and Dad loved about him. Ha! I'm kidding—it drove my parents insane. He is the smartest of all four of us, although Nick will contest that. Tim is sweet and lovely and the kindest of all of us.

Even though around us he would never shut up, as a kid Tim was actually the shyest one of us and would only ever do things if Nick was around. One time, when Tim was about ten, we were at McDonald's—our favourite restaurant (and still mine to this very day)—and he wanted a thirty-cent ice cream cone. Mum gave him the money and told him to go up and buy it. He couldn't do it. He had to take Nick with him, and Nick had to do all the talking and make the actual purchase. These days, Nick is still buying cones for the two of them—just a different type.

Together, Nick and Tim are superhuman, totally unstoppable, but when you get each of them on their own, there is just something missing. Don't get me wrong—they are incredible, but when they *both* put their minds to something, they just go above and beyond anything I could ever expect. They both know that. They are both fully aware of the personality change when they are around each other. And if you thought I was loud, you need to meet the full force of Nick and Tim.

Nick is someone who is so confident and so smart, it sometimes hurts to witness it. He was bright as a kid, but Tim was always that bit better at school. But now Nick is older, he is much smarter than Tim at life. It is so hard to explain and, Tim, if you are reading this, I'm sorry mate, but Nick shits all over you with life advice. I mean, Tim, you have your life totally together and, yes, you are miles ahead of Nick in many things, but Nick can just read a situation and tell you exactly what you need to do and what you need to be careful of. He offers such rock-solid advice that sometimes it is a hard pill to swallow. You want to believe something else but, in the end, he is always right.

Nick gets that trait from Mum. It has taken me years to actually take on board the advice Mum gives me. Growing up, I hated being told what to do and how to live. Mum always had the best of intentions, but I hated it. I wanted to make my own decisions and follow my own path. She always told me which of the options was better and always told me when something was too good to be true. She was never ever wrong, and I HATED THAT SO MUCH! She was always right.

However, these were lessons I needed to learn on my own and now, at twenty-thirteen years of age, I really take on board her advice.

Out of the four of us, Nick also possesses the most annoying qualities. He is forever looking at his phone—he will have a full conversation with you and not look up from his phone once. It drives us all, especially his fiancée, Holly, mental. He is also always busy doing something and whenever I visit, I hardly see him. He and I share that in common: I am often too busy or tired to put in the effort socialising. Sometimes he is the same, and I hate it! It's only okay for me to be anti-social: everyone else has to socialise when I want them to!

If Nick and Tim are two halves of one whole, it is fair to say that Adrian is very much his own person. He is definitely the black sheep of the family, but after his rocky start to life, he turned out okay. He was my arch nemesis growing up—but instead of attempting to out*do* each other, we constantly tried to out-*lazy* each other. Who could get away with doing the least amount of housework and homework and who could watch more TV. It was a Battle Royale, but HE ABSOLUTELY WON! He has an uncanny ability to not hear anything going on around him when the TV is on and he will watch absolutely anything. He once watched four hours of *Rage*, the music countdown show. Seriously, do you not have anything better to do? Even I couldn't sit through four hours of that, and I could represent Australia in the yet to become official (but 2024's a charm!) Olympic sport of tandem TV watching and snacking.

While Tim and Nick were straight-A students, Adrian and I were lucky if we got Cs. We both hated school and thought the routine of learning sucked. It didn't suit us. We weren't booksmart. I was a creative and Adrian is a mechanic who likes to get his hands dirty. School wasn't for us. Although he and I are almost exactly the same in that regard, we are totally opposite in others. I'm gay and a wimp, and he is straight and nothing scares him. Well, except large huntsmen.

When it comes to explaining how Adrian is different from me and Nick and Tim (or as Dad would yell from across the room, 'Nick, Tim and I'), it would be easier to just say that he must have been adopted from Planet Boganite. While I have zero masculinity and Nick and Tim have about forty per cent on a good day, Adrian for some reason inherited one hundred per cent of the typical bloke traits that Nick, Tim and myself missed out on.

Ady couldn't give two shits about most things, has a ute, owned four rifles at one point, has zero interest in fashion and drinks bourbon and coke. And as he is a mechanic, he is constantly covered in grease and shit. He has made a life for himself that we all respect.

I talk to Ady the most out of my brothers, and we have a special bond of sharing stuff we wouldn't tell the others (not that it's a competition but I win, I'm Adrian's favourite). He calls me every now and then to see how I am going and to get the lowdown on the latest disastrous Grindr situations I have got myself into.

Weirdly, my three brothers often seem to me like they are my older siblings. Nick and Tim offer life advice and support and seem to see when I am going off course and guide me back to where I need to be. They probably don't realise they are doing this, but I rely on them. And Adrian is always there, checking in with me and making me feel connected to the family even though I don't live anywhere near them.

I love my brothers. We have never had a big fight, never had a punch-up, never had a real disagreement. I am so lucky to have such a rock-solid family.

Now you know my family and how much they mean to me. They have completely shaped who I am as a person and if you have any issues with the following stories about my life, please direct all hate towards them. It's their fault. If, however, you like the stories and what I am about to tell you, it's all me and I had no help from them.

2

GRAND OLD PARENTS

I was absolutely spoilt rotten as a kid. I realise now that the struggle Mum and Dad went through to finally have a child and the harrowing experience of losing twin boys they endured before having me meant I was a very special gift. I still see myself as the most amazing gift that ever entered my parents' lives, but I'm pretty sure that as the years have gone by, they see me less as the gift that keepeth on giving and more as the gift that keepeth on taking.

Among all of my wonderful, spoilt-rotten memories of childhood, my fondest are of spending time with my grandparents. Flash back thirty(ish) years: my dad's parents, Alan and Joan, are overcome with joy at my birth. My parents weren't spring chickens when they had me, so my grandparents were practically in the crypt by the time I was born.

Seriously, they'd probably begun to think they wouldn't live to see the next generation of their son's family, so when I came along, it was a VERY BIG DEAL.

The earliest memory I have of them is sitting with Nanna Joan at the kitchen table in her home in Berkeley Vale on the Central Coast. Their home was small, but next to a massive park. I would have been four years old. The kitchen table was a light grey with two padded vinyl-covered bench seats. Imagine the seats on a bus or train, but grey. I feel like it must have been a classic eighties IKEA purchase. It was probably fairly basic for the time, but today would be ultra retro-chic. Sitting across from me at this kitchen table was Nanna Joan, with her short white hair, soft flowery dress and big personality. She was super gentle and always had a little gift for me when I arrived—and a packet of Smarties.

In 1993 when I was five, I had my first experience of losing a close family member when Nanna Joan passed away. I don't really remember that much about it, except that it all seemed hectic, rushed and fast. One minute we were visiting her in hospital, and the next we were at her funeral.

I don't remember the service, but I do remember that Enya was the music played. FUCKING ENYA! What a boss. Nanna Joan had specifically asked that Enya be played at her funeral. I think Enya is officially the worst artist in the history of the world to play at a funeral. Instantly, everyone starts bawling and the music is so beautiful and sad that the bawling soon turns to wailing and gnashing of teeth. I'm pretty sure Joan knew what she was doing when she requested Eyna.

I have decided that just like Nanna Joan, I want Enya played at my funeral. Enya is one of the most amazing singers of all time, but to play her at a funeral is a brilliant and brutal last move. Enya makes me cry on a good day. Imagine at a funeral.

I applaud Joan's final checkmate to everyone. Man, that lady had some spunk.

After Joan's death, my grandfather Alan often stayed over at our house. He would have been in his early eighties when she died. My memories of Pa are mostly of him sitting on the couch, a trait I inherited from him. Boy oh boy, if only he could see my world-class couch-sitting skills now, he would be so damn proud.

He was a solid man—not fat, just a bit of a unit. My dad was tall and skinny, but Pa was built. He had white hair and big black-rimmed glasses. Imagine if Colonel Sanders had a burly brother. That's Pa.

In the Hull mansion, we had a huge living room, with one whole wall of glass and some sliding doors that looked into our big backyard. In the living room were two big soft black pleather couches (the height of class back in the day, thank you very much). Pa had his spot and he would sit there, watching the chaos of four boys running amok and Mum and Dad constantly yelling at us. We would often play right at his feet. There would be toys and yelling and fighting and snatching and tears and tantrums, the lot—and Pa would just sit there quietly and watch. We would play dress-ups and force Pa to play with us, which he somehow managed to do from the comfort of his couch. There is an amazing photo of him dressed as a pirate, just sitting in his chair with an eye patch on and a hook for a hand. He was very tolerant.

Occasionally he would yell at us for fighting with each other and grab his walking stick and poke us. He had one of those canes that looked like a wooden gearstick—almost like the one from *Jurassic Park*, but dark wood (and without the million-dollar, dinosaur-life-giving mosquito in the head—he wasn't that out there). It never left his side and I remember him having it at all times. Mostly for protection from us boys.

After Nanna Joan died, Pa lived in a retirement home in the beachside Sydney suburb of Narrabeen. It was an amazing place and he had this tiny unit which was literally only *just* big enough to fit his pride and joy, a recliner. Visiting him as a kid was exactly like when Bart Simpson visits Abe. All the oldies would be obsessed with us and they would come up to us and pat us and pinch us and ask us a million questions. It could be a daunting experience but thankfully we knew a back way to get to Pa's unit without having to encounter too many of the crazy oldies. It felt like a secret stealth mission getting to Pa's and getting out again without anyone spotting us and our pinchable cheeks.

I used to feel sad for Pa. Sitting alone in that room, watching TV. I now realise it is my dream existence, so maybe it wasn't so bad for him after all. In all seriousness, though, I hope it was an enjoyable last few years for him. I can't imagine what it would be like to lose a partner and then be alone in a little unit. I think that's why he was often on our couch, just watching us play. The company was what he liked. The chaos.

In 1998, at the age of eighty-six, he passed away. I was eleven. It was sad of course, but I still didn't really understand the concept of death. At eleven, I knew what had happened, but it wasn't as emotional as losing a grandparent when you are older. It was weird seeing that vacant spot on the couch, though.

My other set of grandparents, Mum's parents George and Leslie, were also super involved in our childhoods and also seriously spoilt us. They had a beautiful home in Lindfield, which was less than half an hour's drive from our house. It was Mum's childhood home and it was so sixties and so fabulous. It felt like the classic grandparents' home.

It was at the very end of the street and down the steepest driveway you could imagine—great for bikes and scooters. If you were standing at their letterbox at the top of the driveway, you could look out and over their roof to the golf course on the other side of the hill. It was super leafy and the driveway was like a cliff leading down to a brown-terracotta tiled carport.

They had a doorbell which I was obsessed with and loved pressing. I would incessantly ring it as much as I could and I was constantly being yelled at for doing so. Once inside their home, it was literally wall-to-wall filled with cool stuff. As you walked in, you were greeted by two enormous rubbings of Chinese warriors. Back in yesteryear, you were allowed to get a piece of paper and rub some charcoal over the figures. Beyond that, you stepped into the fancy adult conversation area—where no kids were allowed, it was called the 'get out of there' room. In that room was the most beautiful glass bowl, which was a deep blue colour and looked like an upside-down octopus. The furniture was so sixties and the carpet was like a big soft shag rug.

The kitchen was off the living room, through some swinging saloon doors. I bloody loved those doors. It felt like a restaurant in the middle of Texas back in the early 1800s. You stepped outside on the full porch that pretty much went all the way around the house and overlooked their pool and an enormous willow tree.

There was this one cupboard in the pool area that was filled with pool toys and goggles. But these were no ordinary goggles. These used to belong to Mum. THEY STILL HAD GOGGLES FROM THE SIXTIES! There was one particular pair that we all wanted to use and would fight over all the time. It was actually a snorkel but was unlike anything you have ever seen. It was a giant oval shape and covered your ENTIRE face, not restricting your view at all. It was something straight out of James Bond and was amazing to swim with. We would fight to the death to use it every time we swam.

This was a home. And it really was like our second home as Nan and Pa would look after us fairly regularly. Maybe because

Mum and Dad needed a break from us on the regular. How and why Nan and Pa continued to look after us so often always boggles my mind. They had raised three girls and now they were looking after four boys. Why the heck would you choose to spend your retirement being tortured by children, when you could instead be curled up in bed with the internet and an endless supply of Caramilk? I just don't understand some people. To be fair, neither of those joys had been invented yet, so I guess there was nothing else to do or eat. Whatever the reason behind their child-caring insanity, we benefited from it, as we always had the best time at their place.

Which brings me to the next retro element of Nan and Pa's house: the food there! It just always tasted different to food we ate anywhere else—not necessarily in a bad way, but it always kinda felt like we were eating war rations at Nan's. Mostly stale chips. I, however, have a love of stale chips. To this day, I will buy a packet of chips, open it and leave it overnight (if I'm not feeling greedy), then eat it the next day. STALE SALT AND VINEGAR IS LIFE! And I know that this love of staleness came from Nan's chips—which she kept above the fridge and which were practically chewy by the time she would hand them out to us. I feel like it is entirely possible that she bought them for Mum when she was a kid and just forgot about them.

Nan also made porridge differently and it was horrible. Mum made porridge with milk, but Nan used water. WHO USES WATER? It was torture to eat and I would sneak into the kitchen and smother it with brown sugar. Was this also a wartime thing? Was she still rationing the milk? And if so, WHY?

And like every good nan, while you ate, you were watched. Not by her, but by the eleven creepy porcelain dolls sitting in several glass cabinets that were built into the wall. Most of the dolls were small, but there was one I called 'Nope'. Nope was pretty much my size and the creepiest doll you'd ever seen. From an early age, I would point at her and simply say, 'Nope'. Nope lived in the cupboard and stayed there. I wanted nothing to do with her. My brothers used to think it was funny to open the cabinet and turn her head slightly, so that when I walked past, it appeared that she had turned her head to watch me, causing me to scream and cry and then rock back and forth in the corner. The movie *Annabelle* is based on my nan's doll collection.

While Nan had her creepy dolls, Pa had the most amazing spoon collection, which was kept in three large wooden spoon display cases also mounted on the wall. Who am I to judge, I love collecting—I have a twenty-eight-piece collection of glass fruit. We had a little ritual where Nan and Pa would make us all a cup of tea, and we would sit up at the table and Pa would let us choose a spoon from the collection to use. It was like Christmas. Picking a single spoon from the 5000 hanging on the wall would take us about six hours, by which time the tea would be cold, but we loved it. Some of the spoons had orna-ments on them and some sported dangly things or pictures of locations. This spoon-choosing process would often also turn into a massive fight because I would see that Nick had his eye on a particular spoon, so I would take it. I never actually wanted that spoon, but I knew Nick did so I was determined he wouldn't get it. I got so much joy from their pain. WHAT A SADISTIC FUCK!

Sadly, the stale chips and large spoon collection are now just memories, as both George and Leslie have passed away. Pa, ever the joker, decided he would leave right on Christmas Day. GREAT JOB! I too hope to leave on a significant day, but I don't think even I can top the magic of Christmas.

3

THE ELDEST
MAKES THE RULES

As I have already said, I love, love, love my brothers. They are my world. They are amazing human beings who I feel lucky to be able to call family.

But, Jesus Christ, they were annoying little shits as kids. And I was even worse.

And I know this for a fact because there is a combined total of roughly 600 years of video footage of the four of us growing up, lovingly captured by my mother (clearly, I got it from her).

In one particular scene in one of these avant-garde filmic masterpieces, Mum has captured my three brothers when they were maybe ten months old. They were fast crawlers. Mum had built a tunnel out of the four billion nappy boxes we went through a week and all three were sprint-crawling through this tunnel. Mum was at one end filming and first you see a shot of Tim, happy as Larry, pop out the end smiling. He stops right there though and doesn't move. Nick is fast coming up behind him and is showing no sign of stopping. Tim, happy and carefree, is then mounted by Nick, who climbs directly over the top of him without even pausing. I am talking right over the top, clawing at his face and his feet kicking poor ole Tim.

That's what it was like every single day. And I don't mean just metaphorically. Like, actually physically crawling over each other and injuring each other to get ahead. Constant competition.

I'll admit that I won most of the time—not due to any particular skill, but rather because I'm a little turd and, being the eldest brother, I would make up rules that worked in my favour. As I mentioned, as kids we were at Nan and Pa's all the time—not because we were devoted grandsons, but because they had an in-ground pool and an endless supply of pool toys. It was at Nan and Pa's that the Real Me would emerge, fully formed and ready to take on the role of the tyrannical, campy, four-foot-tall dictator of the Land of Brothers. Imagine a cross between Liberace and Squidward, that was me.

I had two simple pool rules for my brothers:

1. The eldest gets to use any toy he wants, and
2. At any moment, the eldest can demand the toy a younger brother was using and that toy must be handed over.

They were my legit rules and I enforced them daily. It always ended in tears and with Nan screaming over the porch,

'Christian, let your brothers have a go!' Then I would cry and say that that was a clear breach of the rules. Then Pa would come out and yell, 'Christian, let your brothers have a go!' Then Nan would yell at Pa and they would argue over who was handling the situation.

Nan was always in the pool too. Not for fun, but to do her exercises. She had very bad arthritis and would use empty three-litre juice bottles as weights under water to manage it and keep up her strength. She would push the bottles under the water and around. We didn't understand the arthritis thing back then—we just thought she had lost the plot and was the crazy lady in the corner who we would avoid. That was until we discovered how fun playing with these bottles was.

We used to swim up and steal them from Nan (lovely boys we were), then dive to the bottom of the pool with them, let them go and watch them shoot into the air. Then, like the little shits we were, we worked out how to weaponise them. We would angle them under the water, let go and they would fire out and strike a brother in the face. It was so satisfying. Half the time, the pool was filled with blood from all the broken noses.

I remember inventing another strange but exhilarating game with my brothers at my grandparents' house. It took place in Nan's laundry, which was a small room under the house. It was the size of a small bedroom and didn't have much natural light. And it had a million cupboards and little places to hide.

The game was as follows: one brother would stand outside and count to twenty and the remaining three would go into the laundry and hide. This wasn't your basic game of hide and seek. Oh no no: this, my friends, had a twist. The twist was that at any given moment, one of us would jump out and scare the living shit out of the 'seeker'. Whoever was the first to scare the seeker was the winner and then it would be their turn to count while the rest of us hid again. This game would go for hours. And it would often end in tears, as most of our games did. Usually, because I did something horrible. It builds resilience.

Based on what I've already described about the warfare that was four brothers growing up together, it won't surprise you that we were always in trouble with Mum and Dad and were yelled at a LOT. But the hilarious part was that when yelling at us, Dad could never get our names right—he would always call us the wrong name, often even throwing in the dog's or cat's name too. He would just go through a weird roll call of every name he knew, until—*BINGO*—he'd finally get to the one he needed. For example, he would be watching the news and I would stand right between him and the TV, blocking his view, just for the fun of it. He would get so irrationally irate that his anger would cause him to scream the following: 'Adrian ... Adrian ... move! Tim ... move! Nick! Tiny (our dog)! Whoever you are, move!'

Dad yelled at us so much that it became like white noise to us. Borderline comforting, even. We could be standing there, two feet from him, him screaming bloody murder at us and we just really didn't even notice or care. Then some sort of object would come flying towards us—never anything very harmful, mind you, mostly the TV guide—and only then would we turn around and be like 'WHAT, DAD?' Oh my god, looking back now, I'm surprised he wasn't admitted to a mental institution, we were so infuriating.

Back then, I didn't understand why Dad had such a low tolerance of us. But as an adult myself now, it is quite clear. It's because kids are annoying AF and never listen. They are like the worst possible version of an adult, just in miniature. If you met an adult who behaved like a child, you would instantly hate them. They are assholes with no redeeming features. And trust me, we all know an adult who acts like a spoiled entitled child.

All of which is to say that far from judging my father or holding his treatment of us against him, I now salute him and admire his stance on us as children and I am happy to be just like him. I have ZERO patience for kids. If I tell them not to do something and they do it anyway, I turn into my father. In fact, I would go ahead and say that on reflection my father had a good tolerance level compared to what I now have. I am worse now than he ever was.

It's not that I am scared of children: it's more that I'm scared *for* them. Because they are so dumb. For example, a baby who has just learned to crawl will do just that towards a chest of drawers and grab one, open it and then will grab the top of that open drawer, push it closed and jam their fingers. They could easily repeat this action eight to twelve times before the parents realise that their kid is too stupid to be trusted with a chest of drawers and that they need to move the goddamn drawers out of the playroom. I know that children do this stupid shit, because that literally happened to me as a child. Many times. I actually put my lack of dexterity down to these childhood traumas. Mum, why did it take you so damn long to move the fucking drawers? LOOK AT MY DEFORMED FINGERS!

Kids don't learn their lesson. It takes injury after injury before their tiny brains even begin to suspect that what they are doing will cause grievous bodily harm. Whenever I see an unattended child, I have a mild panic attack. They are just an injury bomb waiting to happen. I don't want to be near or around them at any stage unless they are in the arms of a parent or asleep. It's the only time I feel safe.

Given my complete lack of interest in children, it might come as a surprise for you to learn that when I was nineteen, I decided very spontaneously that I was going to be a camp counsellor in America. For those who don't know, in the States, summer camps are huge—they are a full-blown tradition and literally every kid goes to one. They are all over the country and range from day camps to marathon eight-week long camps.

Remember school camp in Year Six? Well, it's like that, but kids in America do it every year during their summer school holidays. These camps have a bunch of camp leaders/counsellors who run programs and lead activities for the kids every day. Some camps like to have international camp counsellors, and so organise people to travel from overseas locations to these camps. They also sort out visas and insurance and working permits for anyone who wants to take part.

When we were both nineteen, my best friend Ashleigh had signed herself up to CCUSA (Camp Counselors USA), a program where they basically match you to the perfect camp for your personality (and take care of all the annoying paperwork). Ash had been raving about CCUSA and was really excited about her impending trip. She had planned it for about six months and had basically not stopped talking about it that whole time. She said it was something I should do too. Maybe Ash didn't appreciate how minimal my skills with children were and how little I knew about how to act around them. Maybe I didn't either. Either way, whether it was because of FOMO or sheer boredom, I signed up—and, even more surprisingly, was accepted.

When the kids arrived for the first day of camp, I realised I didn't know how to be a responsible leader and also that I had absolutely no authority or control. My years of ordering my brothers around like a stocky sergeant major counted for nothing here. These American kids didn't have that natural fear and subordination that younger siblings do of the eldest child in the family, which I realised had been key to any authority I'd ever wielded. I realised my power was essentially an illusion, a house of cards built on nothing more than birth order.

The kids at camp were awesome, but I felt completely out of place if I had to tell them off. If a child said something inappropriate, mostly I would laugh and then get a glare from another counsellor. It's fair to say I wasn't a model counsellor and that I could most generously be described as being a mild to moderate (at best) success at this whole sorry venture. Others who witnessed this shitshow would probably describe me not as a counsellor, but as another child who the other proper counsellors had to boss around.

My lack of natural ability, however, didn't stop me from signing up to do it for two more summers. One time in particular stands out for me being completely out of my depth. Two other counsellors and I had been put in charge of 'Earwig' (weird name, I know). Earwig was a group of eleven boys between the ages of ten and thirteen. We were in charge of these boys overnight and during the morning. What this entailed was pretty standard: making sure the boys behaved themselves as they showered, brushed their teeth and got ready for bed. Then it would involve repeatedly telling them to shut up and go to sleep. During the day, we'd make sure the boys were up and ready on time and then would take them to breakfast, where all the units would come together. After breakfast, all the kids would branch off into whatever daily activities were on offer, for example, horseriding, making friendship bracelets (by far the most popular one—and my personal favourite), hiking, etc.

But once during every camp, we would have a special 'Unit Day', where your unit would do something special together, just as an individual unit. The counsellors would plan the day, and for Earwig that year we planned to hike to a particular park and have a sleep-out there. Little did I know that this would be the fateful day where I would lose control of the children completely and they would go all *Lord of the Flies* on me.

After cooking dinner on the campfire, we set off for the park. And by 'park', I mean the forest, as the camp was located deep in the Californian redwood reserve. I was accompanied by my two fellow counsellors, whose identities I will not reveal for legal reasons. Why? Because they screwed me over big time. Just before we were due to set off, they sprung it on me that I would be sleeping out with the boys on my own while they stayed back and had sex all night. Excusez-moi! What the actual fuck?!

Their sex plan was that one of them—let's call him Owen (because his name was Owen)—would stay back at base camp and offer to wash all the dishes while myself and Owen's co-conspirator, let's call her Sally (yep, that is her real name too), took the boys to where we would be sleeping for the night. Once we were settled at our designated sleep site, Sally would make an excuse to go back to base camp for sexy time. Thus leaving me alone looking after eleven hyperactive, batshit-crazy, pre-adolescent boys. Selfish, irre-sponsible, reprehensible heterosexuals.

So, that's what happened. Sally left and, for a time, everything seemed to be going okay. The boys were angels and there wasn't any trouble. That was up until bedtime. Once they were all in sleeping-bags, something clicked and they instantaneously went from being angels to actual devils. They began to ask each other unbelievably inappropriate questions. Without Sally or Owen to help me shut this shit down, I was on my own and out of my depth.

Some of their (frankly, kind of impressive) questions included: 'What's a dildo?', 'How many holes does a woman have?', 'Do you know what golden showers are?' and the old classic handed down through generations of horny young boys, 'Do you watch porn?'

I was dying on the inside.

I tried my best to shut it down. 'Guys,' I said. 'These questions are not appropriate for the group.'

But there was a slightly older boy—maybe thirteen years old—in the group who knew far too much and he kept answering everything. If I'm honest, even I learned a thing or two from him that night. But that's beside the point.

I couldn't handle it. I was so uncomfortable. The question that caused me to stand up and threaten that if they didn't stop, we would all be hiking back to base camp was, 'What's jizz?'

THAT WAS IT! I WAS DONE!

'Boys, you need to stop!' I yelled.

They were all in hysterics. They were loving how awkward I was.

It's also worth noting that these boys were not as dumb as they seemed—they'd also quickly realised what Owen and Sally were up to and tried to get me to confirm it. Of course, I denied it all and told them that Sally has just lost a very close family member and Owen was making sure she was okay (with his penis). Well done to quick-thinking Christian! I remember being quite proud of that off-the-cuff lie. And it worked a treat until we all got back to the base camp the next day and the boys offered Sally their condolences.

Another year at camp, I was placed in charge of the youngest girls unit: there were eight seven- to nine-year-olds. They were all bloody divine and super cute. On the first night, around the campfire, one of them whispered loudly—a comedic yelling whisper like they do in over-the-top Broadway musicals—'Is that man gay?' She was seven years old! To her credit, my choice of outfit was a bit of a dead giveaway: multi-coloured knee-high socks, terry towelling shorts and a fluoro T-shirt—all topped off with a Glomesh bumbag. BUT HOW DID SHE KNOW?

I guess what my thoughts about children really boil down to is that in the child–adult dynamic, I am completely uncomfortable playing the adult. Having three brothers and spending years as a camp counsellor has shown me that when I see kids, I recognise them for the annoying little shits they are. And I relate to that more than I do to being the authority figure who has to manage that behaviour. Frankly, I'd rather join in the madness than try to stop it. And while I can freely admit that on the very odd occasion they can be adorable, this is something I am mostly quite happy to admire from a distance.

The truth is that I love my child-free life.

4

HIGHS AND LOWS

I'm not that intelligent. I'm fine with this news. It doesn't bother me. I don't have a job that requires a high level of intelligence. I'm lucky enough to be gifted with a creative brain. So, it won't come as any surprise to you (especially those of you who are parents) that I struggled throughout school. It started off okay. Day one, lots of photos of adorable little Christian in his cute school uniform and enormous backpack (what the fuck was in there, Mum?), posing next to a tree, posing at the front door, posing by the letterbox—if it existed, I posed next to it. The triplets were somewhere in the background being neglected as I lapped up the limelight. As soon as we got to the gate, however, I changed my mind, decided I hated school and cried for Mum. Almost nothing has changed.

I quickly learned that I related more to the girls in my class than to the other boys and I became a ladies' man. I was teased because of it, but that didn't bother me too much because I was just so damn popular with the girls. I made it my mission to make them laugh and when they did, it filled me with so much pleasure. Who would have thought that the ladies would bring me pleasure!

I was confident, popular, polite and funny as well. However, one of my downsides was my sporting ability. Even though I was a skinny little athletic-looking kid, I sucked at doing anything sport related. Other than that my lack of sporting prowess—which, let's face it, is practically the currency that school runs on—I got by okay in infants school, probably because in Kindergarten through to Year Three, the hardest things you had to do were trace letters of the alphabet and read books about cats jumping into hats.

But by the time I was in about Year Four, the classroom stepped up to an advanced level of learning and it became kind of clear that academia and I weren't exactly a match made in heaven. I wasn't a disaster, but I wasn't great either. I wasn't a good reader, speller or achiever and was generally just a little below average. I struggled to concentrate in class and had started to fall behind the other students in my work. On reflection, it was at about this time that my schooling got too far ahead of me and I was unable to catch up.

As I was my parents' first child, they thought maybe they were doing something wrong, so they decided to get me tested to figure out whether it was them or me. Spoiler alert: it was them, obviously—how dare they make me dumb! I was nine when I was marched into a house that had been converted into a child psychologist's clinic. I was there for one reason: to determine if I had learning issues.

It was actually a pretty fun place—there were puzzles and toys everywhere. I played around for a bit and after a while Mum, Dad and I were called in to see the man we had come to see. He was very friendly and smiled a lot. He mostly talked to my parents, so I zoned out and wasn't really paying attention. Classic Christian: off in my own world.

After that, I had to do an IQ test. I quite enjoyed it, to be honest. I had to solve different word puzzles and maths problems and describe shapes and other fun stuff.

In the end, I remember being told that I had a super high IQ and that I was fine. But looking back on it now, I'm sure they were totally lying to me and that in fact I had a low IQ and the 'tears of happiness' from my mother were in fact tears of sadness. She had a dud son.

I ended up getting some extra help with my reading and writing and maths, and things kind of levelled out from there. I managed to scrape through as a bit below average and everyone stopped freaking out.

Other than this episode with the child psychologist, primary school was pretty straightforward. I made some great friends (all girls—yes, every single one of them) and got along well with my teachers. In fact, I still hold the school record for being teacher's pet for seven consecutive years throughout primary school. What can I say? I was adorable! I had an impressive Tazo collection (which would be worth ones of dollars today) and I learned clarinet and piano—a fact that would ultimately lead to me meeting my BFF in high-school band, but I didn't know any of that back then.

When I was in Year Five, my little brothers also started at the same school, and took an enormous amount of attention away from me. I don't know what it is, but people love triplets! Take it from me because I can tell you: they are nothing special at all. I was livid. It was at this moment that I knew I would have to work to regain my popularity and claw back the attention I had lost to them, a realisation that actually set me on a course to becoming school captain. Move over, Machiavelli!

One more thing you should know about me and primary school: I was the shortest kid at my school. No, I did not miswrite that—no, I did not mean to say 'in my class'. I mean in my whole fucking school. The kindergarten kids were taller than me. Five-year-olds taller than an eleven-year-old.

School photos were always fun. The whole class picture was always the one I looked forward to the most (sarcasm). The photographer would get us all together and I would always be standing in the second row behind the girls who were sitting. I was always on the end and I was always standing on not one but two blocks. I was so short that if they didn't have me standing on two blocks, I would ruin the aesthetics of the photo. Everyone would laugh and I would laugh too but I was dying on the inside. I couldn't wait for my growth spurt. Another spoiler alert: it never came.

Despite the annual mortification that was photos day, overall I was a pretty happy and confident kid throughout primary school. Even though I was, as the other kids would say, 'vertically challenged' (btw, that was *never* funny and still isn't and if you ever say those words to my face as an adult, you'll win an instant holiday to my shit-list), I was never really seriously bullied and pretty much cruised through unscathed.

In Year Six, I even achieved the ultimate in popularity by being elected school captain. IMPRESSIVE! Let's gloss over the fact my school was one of the smallest schools in Australia with about 120 kids and that in my class there were only five boys. Glossing, glossing, glossing right over those boring details. School captain: YAY! Triplets who?

I also, perhaps perplexingly, was cast as the lead part of 'Sandy' in a school production of *Grease* once. For an equally confusing and unknown reason, it wasn't even a singing role, it was just one scene of dialogue and a bit of dancing. Why did I, a short smiley boy, play the coveted main female part of Sandy, you may ask? I have no idea! It does seem quite ludicrous! I know the concept of me donning a cheap blonde wig and adopting the personality of a woman sounds absolutely INSANE. Flash forward twenty years, I still have that blonde wig.

I think a huge amount of credit for my primary school years being happy and fun needs to go to my mum and dad:

the fact is, I was loved for who I was. So while I wasn't ever perfect and I had my issues like most kids do, it was never the sole focus and it never made me feel like I wasn't enough. As a family we were close and loving, and to this day I am grateful that I had the family that I did as my foundation, who helped shape me into who I am as I grew up.

Unfortunately, in high school, everything unravelled. The carefree days of primary school were gone and everything stepped up about 60,000 notches. My Year Seven class was the size of my entire primary school. I went from a school of 120 to a school of 1200.

Being small, overwhelmed and a little different automatically made me a target. I learned this pretty quickly. The first episode I recall took place early in my first year of high school during a fitness test. The entire Year Seven class had to complete a fitness course, which involved running timed laps of the oval. I was on my fourth lap of the 400-metre track and I was exhausted and jogging slowly. Fitness let me down yet again.

There I was, trotting along and minding my own business, daydreaming of a caramel-flavoured white chocolate that hadn't been invented yet, when up behind me came three boys from my class who I barely knew. These boys proceeded to jog slowly behind me, calling me names and saying some pretty horrific things for the couple of minutes it took for me to finish the lap. A few minutes had not ever felt so long before and has not ever since. One of them finished by saying he was going to beat me up so badly that my mum wouldn't even recognise me.

What a little piece of shit! What an actual piece of human garbage. Who in their right mind would ever think that's an appropriate thing to say? I didn't interact with the bullies— I just tried to ignore them, finished the jogging course and rejoined the rest of the class.

But from that moment on, high school totally changed for me. I retreated into my shell and hid myself away as much as I could. I wasn't my true self. After that experience on the oval, I knew that my personality couldn't ever come out. If I revealed the real me like I had in primary school, I knew I wouldn't survive high school.

So, I spent every lunchtime in the library on my own, hiding up the back at one of the corner desks doing homework. I rarely participated in class and I did not get involved in any extra-curricular activities for the whole first year. I had come to the understanding that the next six years were going to be hard. I resigned myself to a high school career of lunching in the library, and even sitting away from people on the bus to and from school.

I still find it sad that I had to change who I was just to make it through school. I don't regret it, though, as what it came down to was almost like survival mode. If I hadn't changed who I was and retreated into the shadows, then I think high school would have been absolute hell for me.

Every now and then I would hang out with two guys from my grade at recess or after school. They were the smartest two boys in my year and were lovely guys, but they were a bit nerdy and socially awkward and they just weren't really my kind of people. Still, we were able to have some laughs and I am thankful that they accepted who I was, and that I was able to be myself around them. Tim and Justin, if you do end up reading this book, I am so thankful for your friendship during my time at St Pat's!

In Year Eight, a bright spot appeared on the horizon when I joined the school band. Band practice was every Wednesday evening and it was something—the only thing, really—that I looked forward to each week. I adored our band leader Mrs Ciampa, who was pale-skinned with heaps of red hair—she was the most Irish person ever, just without the accent. The band was a large group of about thirty amazingly awesome kids who I could finally be myself around. Thank god my parents had sent me to clarinet lessons in primary school, as that little ole woodwind instrument damn well saved my life in high school.

I sat up the very front playing the clarinet alongside Josephine, who was in the year above me. Fuck, we had fun. We never socialised in the playground but during band rehearsals we had the best time. She was loud and zany, and we would do the funniest shit. We had many in-jokes. No one else in my grade was in the band, until one day a new member joined. Ashleigh was a shy saxophone player who sat towards the back. I knew that she was in my grade, but we had never spoken before. From memory, it was a while before we really connected in band too. I don't remember how it happened, but we became close over a period of time, a closeness that led us to be best friends. Which we have been ever since.

Ash and I really grew close in years Eleven and Twelve, as we did a few subjects together: maths, art and music. During maths, we would plan our lives together. We would obviously be wealthy and own a three-storey home on Sydney Harbour. Ashleigh would have her own storey, which would contain a tattoo studio, as she wanted to be a tattoo artist, and my private storey would have a radio studio, as I was going to be the next Kyle Sandilands (then and now, a famous and very successful radio host) when I grew up. We would also have an incredibly cool rooftop for parties. Fast-forward fifteen years and Ashleigh and I are now both over thirty years of age but are literally no closer to achieving this than we were when we first came up with the idea in high school.

So, while our heads might have been in the clouds, I can safely say that without Ashleigh and the school band, I would not have enjoyed my time at St Pat's at all. I eventually made a few other friends, too, and by Year Eleven, lunchtimes in the library were mostly a thing of the past. Mainly thanks to Ashleigh, I guess I came out of my shell a tiny bit. Not fully out, but enough to make some decent memories. It's amazing what a wingman—or in my case, a wingwoman—can do. That's my advice to anyone struggling through high school or any other situation: really, all it takes is one friend to get you started. Once you have that person, things won't automatically become one hundred per cent perfect, but with that person, you will get through.

Another friend I made in senior school was Chantelle. We became friends because we had homeroom together every morning. She was a tall loud redhead who wasn't afraid of anything, and I think we clicked as we shared a similar (sick) sense of humour.

Chantelle would get on the school bus at one of the first stops every day and would claim a good spot up the back. A few stops later, I would get on and go sit with her. One day in Year Eleven while on the bus, Chantelle asked if I would wag school with her that day. Now, I was not the type to wag school, but I loved hanging out with Chantelle and we always had the best time, so . . . I was on board!

We got off the bus a few stops early, at Eastwood station. By then, the bus was already half full of other kids from school who, when they saw us getting off, knew exactly what we were doing. I felt so goddamn cool. I could hear them whispering and see them pointing. I felt so rebellious.

This wasn't the first time Chantelle had wagged school, mind you—she was a pro at this. She knew exactly what she was doing and I loved it. After we got off the bus, we went to the Go-Lo store in the plaza at Eastwood. This was a massive store that sold everything and it was cheap. The plan was to go in, get a bunch of lollies and have a feast in the park nearby.

When I say get a bunch of lollies, I should clarify that we had no money and we were going to shoplift them. I felt like Tom Cruise in *Mission Impossible*. We strutted inside and just went to town. Chantelle had a foolproof theft system that for legal reasons I am not able to share with you. She was the master. Like, actual master. I wasn't too bad, but nowhere near as good as her. Long story short: we got the gear, walked out of Go-Lo and headed with our loot to the park. We sat down and feasted on unique Asian lollies and Pringles. Turns out it actually *was* a tube of Pringles in my pants, I wasn't just happy to see you.

The idea was to then make our way to school and just sneak into class like nothing had happened. We did just that and we had totally got away with it. UNTIL . . . 'Christian Hull, please report to the principal's office' came over the loudspeaker.

Holy mother of Christ! We had been caught! In a fit of panic, I made my way to the principal's office to await expulsion. I was terrified. The first time I had ever wagged and now it was going to end me.

I was marched in to see the principal. He was very polite and didn't seem upset or angry. (It is worth mentioning that at the time my mother was on the payroll at the school as a teacher's aide and I remain confident that this is the only reason I wasn't suspended.) He simply asked why I was late to school that morning and in true Christian Hull style, I made up the lamest, most unbelievable excuse ever.

I was put on the spot and had to think of an answer quickly and this was the story I came up with: 'I'm so sorry about being late, but on my way to catch the bus I tripped over and hurt myself so I went back home to clean myself up and missed the first bus back and had to make my way to school on a different bus that went a different way and then I got off that bus because I didn't know where I was and I walked the rest of the way to school.'

What a story! One Pulitzer Prize coming my way. He said nothing for a while and then just warned me never to let it happen again. I knew he knew that I was lying. I was—and still am—the worst liar in the world. Another good example of me unsuccessfully lying through my teeth was when being constantly asked if I was gay. My answer was always to screech with my limp wrists in the air, 'No, darl, of course I love . . . what do you call them? . . . Oh, GIRLS!'

I obviously didn't take our principal's advice and wagged school a bunch more times with Chantelle. I also went through a terrible kleptomania phase after that. I ended up getting caught by my parents and made to return all the stuff I stole.

So, in the end, despite a pretty bad start, I did end up having some good times at St Pat's. My academic career was never a highlight, but I completed Year Twelve and got my Higher School Certificate, mostly because it was important to my parents. Because for the career that I was planning, which was 'mooching off my parents forever', I was definitely not going to need it.

I made it through mostly okay, but at the end of the day, school wasn't designed for a kid like me. In fact, I would question whether it really caters for most kinds of kids these days. What life skills do they teach? WHEN HAVE YOU EVER USED FUCKING ALGEBRA? Pythagoras, sit down and shut up. There's more to life than goddamn triangles.

Instead, I wish there were classes in public speaking and creative writing. Not generic English where you learn the basics. But subjects like screenwriting and intensive courses you can take in years Eleven and Twelve. I totally understand that's a pipedream and a big ask, but I do think schools need to start offering a diverse range of things instead of forcing kids who aren't cut out for it to just do maths and English.

The only classes I enjoyed were art and music. They were the two classes I actually did well in but they count for almost nothing in the final mark you get, which determines your score to get into university.

I was lucky in that from Year Eleven on, I knew university wasn't for me. I didn't want to go and I didn't want to keep studying after school. My parents never forced the issue, probably because they could also see I was passionate about something else: radio. I volunteered at a few stations and I worked a full-time job at one too. In fact, you could say that school was actually my side hustle.

The fact that I had this whole other life outside of school that tapped into my interests is ultimately what got me through. At school, I was average at best and pretty shy, with only a few good friends. But at the radio stations I worked and volunteered at I was confident and part of the gang and I knew my shit. I reckon if every kid who struggles at school had the chance to pursue something alongside school that they actually cared about, everyone would end up better off: the kids, the school, the teachers and society in general.

5

LESBIAN ISLAND AKA THE ISLE OF LESBOS

I am not one to seek out or surround myself with close relationships—be it friendships or partners, relationships are just not my priority in life. I am very much someone who keeps to themselves—I love my own space and I am not willing to compromise that. I have been like that my entire life.

An example of this is when a group of friends and I rented a holiday house on the coast for a week a few years ago. I took a tent to set up in the backyard and sleep in because I wanted my own space. I didn't want to share a room, let alone a bed, or sleep on the couch. I took a fucking tent to sleep in the backyard. A place I could retreat to and just relax. Who does that? I was the laughing-stock of the trip but I bloody loved it.

But even a hardcore introvert like me needs some friends. Just not very many. And they have to be the highest possible calibre of friend for me to be able to put up with them. And they absolutely cannot be needy as fuck either. I got lucky. I have managed to track down the best three people in the whole world and have personally ordained them into the inner circle of Christianity. That doesn't sound right. Christianism? Or the Church of Hullarity. Let's go with that one.

I don't socialise with them all that much, and I also don't talk to them as often as I should. I am a very solo person—I live alone, and I'll more than likely die alone. God, that sounds bleak, but that's just who I am as a person. I live my life though Facebook: I make funny videos and that's what I enjoy doing.

An average day for me can involve no actual face-to-face contact with anyone. Posting videos, reading comments and responding online could be my entire social life for weeks, and I'd be happy with that. I have no problem not leaving the house and only do so when I absolutely have to. Of course, I talk to my family on the phone now and again, but even they know not to bug me too much.

This doesn't mean that the friends I have are not important to me, though—they are. I have already mentioned Ashleigh, who I became friends with through school band and who remains my best friend to this day—we have so far clocked up close to twenty years of friendship and I am one hundred per cent confident we have at least another couple of decades ahead of us (assuming I don't kill her due to my growing frustration with her soft talking). My friendship with Ashleigh is basically my ideal: it is both the real deal *and* unbelievably low maintenance, and that's how we both like it. We literally live in different countries now and talk about once a year.

When we first met, however, we didn't click straight away—it took a little bit of time for us to connect and we were not instantly best friends. This is probably due to the fact that Ashleigh and I couldn't be more opposite—we are very different types of people. Ash is really quiet, very calm and, although I didn't know this when we first became friends, she is a lesbian. What is it with the gays?! We just seem to attract each other—and not in a physical way.

The most striking difference between us is our volume. I am always at one hundred per cent—I am so loud that my voice actually distorts. Ashleigh is the most annoyingly quiet talker of all time. It is her most irritating trait and I am forever asking her to repeat herself or rudely shouting 'HUH?' at her. I think I might have made myself a bit deaf due to how loud I am—my hearing is bad on a good day. Having a conversation with Ash is like sticking pins not only in your eyes but also in your dick. SPEAK UP, ASHLEIGH!

But despite her being vocally challenged (WE ARE NOT IN A LIBRARY OR A CHURCH, ASHLEIGH, SPEAK THE FUCK UP!), we ARE best friends, I think. I mean, she did feel the need to flee to Los Angeles, but I am ninety-nine per cent sure that was for her work. She is pretty much a famous photographer over there now. She left the country to pursue her passion for photography and from what she tells me, she is doing really well. She was recently one of only very few people to be accepted into a super exclusive and fancy photography course in America where the teachers are mega famous photographers themselves. Her works are extremely cool and postmodern.

Back in school, Ashleigh and I didn't ever hang out outside of school, but we just had this bond. I guess for the first few years of knowing her, I was still pretty closed off: my experiences in high school had taught me to keep to myself—and it's hard to make close friends when you're hiding in the library every lunchtime. But Ashleigh and I slowly and steadily got to know each other better during band practice and I started to relax and be myself around her.

By Year Twelve, we were sitting together in class and hanging out at recess and lunch, too. I still wasn't the fully formed Christian that the internet world now knows, but I was definitely getting closer. Ashleigh was effectively my first test audience, and I would essentially 'perform' for her day in, day out, making stupid jokes and generally trying to be entertaining and loud and fun and to make her laugh nonstop.

We also bonded over our mutual hatred of sport! Every Thursday was sports day at our school. The only semi-good thing about sports day was that we got to wear a sports uniform to school that day—it was the most eighties and puffy yet uber-comfortable uniform in the world. Think Kath Day-Knight, but in green and yellow. From Year Seven to Year

Ten, on Thursdays, I was forced to participate in a variety of sports. It was the worst. First, I did badminton (note, it is not called goodminton and there is a reason for that), but then they added tenpin bowling, so that was a win. I did bowling all through Year Ten, but by the time Year Eleven rolled around, I was fed up. Even bowling was too sporto for me. Ashleigh was fed up too. We were so repulsed by sporting activities that we devised a plan to permanently get out of sports day.

Ash and I, along with a few other band friends, decided to pitch the idea of doing band practice during sport time. The pitch went well and the principal and music teachers totally bought the idea. Every Thursday from then on, we would do a few classes then spend the afternoon dodging sport and pretending to learn and practise our music. We honestly did nothing during this time. We just socialised and had the best time. We thought we were so smart until the day the principal asked us to perform during an assembly. PERFORM! What were we going to perform?? We had been skil-fully dodging sport for six months now but we had done no practice, we had no arrangements together, we had nothing.

We were fucked. Like actually fucked. There were about seven of us in this little sport-avoidant group, and once the request was made, we had to go through with it. We all got up and performed as a group at assembly in front of the entire school. It was the worst day of my life and we sucked so bad. We were so horrific. We literally got up there and just did some jamming together and it sounded like cats dying. Imagine a baritone saxophone, a clarinet, a flute, a singer and keyboards. I ONY WISH WE HAD FOOTAGE OF IT! It was like something from a sitcom and we never lived that performance down.

In years Eleven and Twelve, I think my newfound confidence in myself was due to the fact that by then, I had formed a few solid friendships—mostly thanks to this group of fellow sport avoiders—and this meant I just stopped giving a shit about fitting in. It's funny because all it takes is having a few cool people in your corner to get you out of the corner, but you have to leave the corner first. It's the ultimate catch-22 situation, where the thing you really need is the exact thing just out of your reach. I am so lucky that I had school band, which put Ashleigh in my corner without me ever having to leave it.

I am so proud of everything she has done—moving to LA and getting married are huge and amazing achievements. I can't wait until we are in our fifties, living the high life and being posh in our adjoining multi-storey mansions on the water in Balmain. THE DREAM IS STILL ALIVE!

Ashleigh came into my life when I was avoiding all human contact and was very much a scared introvert, yet to explode out into the world. Funnily enough, she was also the catalyst for me signing up to be a camp counsellor in America, which is where I met my other BFF. Until Ashleigh brainwashed me, camp had never interested me. I was happy in the safety of my home, with Mum and Dad doing everything for me. I had a full-time job and I was earning a bit of money. But I was feeling stale and my life hadn't moved forward as much as I wanted it to since finishing school.

It was April 2006, and I was still finding myself. I'd been working full-time in retail and customer service and it was driving me completely crazy. Working in retail had made me hate people. Customers are actual dicks and I hate them so much. 'Cunts-tomers' was how I would refer to most of them (behind their backs). I feel like everyone should work in retail or hospitality for a stage of their life. It makes you understand just how petty, rude and entitled the human race can be. A huge chunk of my disdain for others comes from my retail experience. If it wasn't for the insanely fun team I worked with, I would have torched the Macquarie Centre within weeks.

I was at a point in my life where I wasn't where I thought I'd be and I wanted more. I was still a virgin (and would be for another three years) and was basically a bit of a loser who pretty much went to Macca's Drive Thru every day and hid in my room for the rest of the time. Was this it?

One night, inspired by Ash's extreme enthusiasm for the program and my own pathetic life, I decided to google CCUSA and just *explore* the option of maybe considering maybe signing up for the following year. Maybe I could go to one of those camps for the uber-wealthy and I could be the indoor counsellor! I noticed on the website the words: 'Cut-off date for applications closes in five days'. They were still taking applications for the upcoming summer. I remember thinking that

I should give it more thought and probably discuss this whole idea with my parents before I applied. If I was going to go, it would be for three months and that was a big deal—also, I couldn't just up and leave my full-time job.

But in a snap impulsive moment (I blame the manipulative 'cut-off date' threat on the website), I just decided that this was something I wanted to do and applied online then and there. A little while later, I had an interview with CCUSA in the city, which I attended without telling anyone, after which I was matched to a camp in California. My visa was organised really quickly, and I went the US Embassy in Sydney to finalise it. It was approved and everything was set.

Except me! By this time, I was due over at camp in about two weeks! SHIT! I needed to tell work and my parents. Work wasn't entirely thrilled but let me take the leave without having to resign. Mum and Dad didn't really seem fazed by my rapid decision to up and leave—I think they were excited to have a break from me for three months.

I booked my ticket and, two weeks later, I flew out to the camp that CCUSA thought I would be a good match with. The camp was called Plantation Farm Camp and it was in a redwood forest near the coast in California. Now here is the kicker, it was an actual working farm. I was matched to a farm camp. I, Christian Hull, was actually matched to an outdoor camp with animals. And we thought Facebook's algorithms were flawed. I'd had an in-depth interview that CCUSA claimed they would use to perfectly match me with a camp that was a synonymous fit. ME! CHRISTIAN! FARM CAMP! I hate animals, I hate the outdoors and I got A FARM CAMP!

According to CCUSA's email, this camp was 'perfect' for me and they were right—if by 'perfect' they meant my worst goddamn nightmare. When I arrived in California after the flight from absolute hell, I made my way to the arranged meeting place for my transfer, which was a very empty carpark opposite a Taco Bell—essentially the perfect location for a serial killer to lure victims to. There, I was greeted by a young guy who pulled up in an SUV—which was covered in dirt and cow shit and had a window missing—who asked in a mumbled Kiwi accent if I was Christian.

Ninety per cent of me wanted to say, 'Hell no' and run away back home and pretend this sorry business had never happened. But I had just survived a flight that I'd thought I was going to die on, so using the logic that I'd already cheated death once on this trip, I decided to try to make it two from two. The young guy loaded my suitcase into the back tray and then it was off to camp—a ninety-minute drive to the middle of fucking nowhere. How fun and safe and completely unscary! Not at all like the start of an American adaptation of *Wolf Creek* . . .

The young guy who had collected me, James, was a softly spoken, skinny, tall and shaggy New Zealander who I would ultimately find out was absolutely divine and a really lovely guy. However, I did not know this at the time, and between

his extreme mumbling and his Kiwi accent and the flapping garbage bag that was covering the missing car window,
I couldn't make out a single word he said to me on that whole
drive. As we drove one hundred kilometres an hour down the
windiest highway on a cliff, he mumbled questions I couldn't
hear, the garbage bag flapped loudly and I started to panic.
I must have said 'Pardon?' about 905 times before I decided
to just guess what he was asking me. WHY DO I ATTRACT
SOFT TALKERS WHO I CANNOT HEAR? This is how a typical
conversation went on that drive:

James: Bfkwo fcjkw swdfj sister sdlkfj at home?
Me: Pardon?
James: Do you dfjk wsedfjj sdfjlk?
Me: Yes, global roaming.
James: Blank stare.
Me: Eyes on the road, buddy!

I wanted to make a good first impression, but I just had
no idea what he was saying. I think at one stage he asked if
I had ever been to the States before and I replied, 'New South
Wales.'

We finally pulled into Plantation Farm Camp after what
seemed like an eternity and my first impression of the camp
was straight-up Manson family ranch. Earlier that year I had
read the book *Helter Skelter*, about the mass murderer Charles
Manson. He lived on a ranch and it was identical to where we
had just pulled up. It was at this moment that I suffered my

first panic attack. Thank the heavens that, despite appearances, Plantation Farm Camp ended up being a lot friendlier and much less murdery than the Manson family ranch.

I got out and was introduced to the other counsellors, and immediately felt so welcomed that all my fears about travelling alone and being away from home instantly disappeared. I was given a tour of the farm, which was huge and a little intimidating: not only was it a working farm, but to top it all off, there was no hot water, no flushing toilets and the only indoor space was the barn. The counsellors slept in three-by-three metre canvas platform tents, which were actually surprisingly cosy and at night we had to use torches (which I quickly learned were called flashlights) to find our way around.

Again, I just want to make sure you appreciate the situation properly: I was interviewed and matched with a camp that had NO INDOORS, NO RUNNING WATER, NO FLUSHING TOILETS AND ANIMALS EVERYWHERE. My personality—the personality of being a spoilt, non-sporty, couch-dwelling lazy bones—was actually matched to this camp. Whatever matching system they used on me, it was broke. I still wonder to this day which question it was that so scrambled the matching system. When I had described myself as pretty hardcore camp, I had meant hardcore fabulous, not hardcore with no electricity.

One thing that was clear to me before I arrived was CCUSA's drug and alcohol policy for counsellors: they absolutely drilled into you that it was illegal to drink if you were under twenty-one and they really put the fear of deportation into you if you so much as even looked at alcohol. And don't get me started on drugs!

And this is where the story gets good. The kids were not arriving at the camp for another week and we were to spend that time setting everything up. Building the tents, getting the kitchen ready and organising the art shack. After an intense first day of setting up, I ate dinner with the team (about fifteen of us) and then, after dinner, two counsellors I had got to know during the day told me to follow them. Keep in mind: this was a farm where the moon and torches were the only light sources. We walked for a while, trudging over a little hill and into what seemed to be dense bushland, quite hidden from view. THIS WAS THE END! I was to be murdered Charles Manson-style and my story would become a movie. The only cold comfort I could take was the sure knowledge that my character would be played by Danny DeVito.

They led me into a small clearing and we sat down in a circle facing each other. I was in full panic mode but managed to maintain a calm exterior. I wasn't thinking 'Flight or fight!?', I was just thinking FUUUUCK! Was I about to be murdered, or had these two girls totally misread me and wanted to have a three-way? They were gorgeous girls, but I think I would have preferred murder.

Then one of the girls pulled out a pipe and that's when it hit me. This was the moment that my twelve years of schooling had been leading me to: a moment where I would either do something to fit in or politely decline. It was a weed pipe— is that even what you call it? The two counsellors had a puff and then it was my turn. They looked at me expectantly.

In that moment, a million things were racing through my head—from anti-drug campaigns we'd done at school to images of US prisons I'd seen on TV. I was torn. I wanted to fit in, but I had never smoked before and there was no way I wanted to try the pipe and then cough and look like a fool. I also didn't want to be uncool or a loser by saying no. It had been a good day and I liked these people and, with three months ahead, I didn't want to start out on the wrong foot with them. This is what was going through my head: *OMG! Just be cool. Just a small puff. No, you'll be deported. Is this a test?*

The time came and I made my decision.

I said no. It was fucking awkward. But I was proud. I was also embarrassed and slightly annoyed that these two people had put me in this position. I was worried that now they would think I wasn't fun and outgoing. I was worried that they would hate me and never talk to me again and it would be the worst three months of my life. Thank GOD, this was not the case. They respected my decision. And funnily enough, I later found out that they had freaked out when I said no and were convinced that I was going to dob on them and get them kicked out. That was also hurtful! I would never do that! Maybe surprisingly, I ended up forming super close relationships with them both and we ended up having that three-way. JOKES! We had an amazing three months working together, but no sexy times. In the end, they weren't half-bad for a pair of stoners.

A few days in, once I had calmed down a little and recovered from the illicit drugs/peer pressure episode, I quickly realised that the people at Plantation Farm Camp were actually amazing and welcoming and so nice, and right off the bat I formed one of the strongest relationships that I have in my life to this day. Trudy. We met on my first day at that summer camp and she has been ingrained in my life ever since. She is one of my closest friends.

When I first saw Trudy, she was wearing overalls, a straw hat and was chewing on some wheat—aka she looked like a complete redneck/bogan. If I'd seen her on the street, I would have crossed the road to avoid her. However, she was super friendly and approached me and LITERALLY said, 'G'day, mate.' She was so Aussie! I had never encountered someone so bogan before. She even said, 'How's it garn?', like an American doing a bad job of playing an Aussie in a C-grade film. Her rural Queensland accent was so thick that I honestly thought it was put on. It wasn't.

When Trudy came along, she entered my life at a really important time. I was discovering who I was and who I wanted to be. She was twenty-seven and I was nineteen when we first met, so she was instantly like an older sister. She is one of the kindest and most understanding humans I have ever met and she has taught me everything I know about being a nice person (which may be a little or a lot, depending on who you ask).

Just like with Ashleigh, I think there is some kind of opposites attract rule at play when it comes to me and Trudy. She is tolerant, accepting and carefree, where I am intolerant, completely judgemental and, let's face it, pretty uptight. Her carefree attitude annoys the absolute fuck out of me because she thinks other people are also nice and carefree. NO, WE ARE NOT!

An example of her carefree attitude is that sometimes she believes the rules don't apply to her . . . like, she is just so laidback that she doesn't pay too much attention to rules she considers petty. Nothing major, just small rules like not bringing outside food into a cinema. She would be like, 'Nah, I'll be fine, I'll just hide it in this obvious food bag.' Into the movies we would go and just like I would have warned her, she would get stopped at the entrance and we would both be punished for her carefreeness.

I adore her.

When we first met at camp, Trudy was very quick to tell me all about her partner, Jen. They'd known each other since high school and had recently become official. They were best of best friends and it was gross. Letters to each other, all that lovey-dovey shit I don't care for. Jen and I met a few months after I'd met Trudy and we got on and continue to get along like a house on fire. We love nothing more than bitching about life and complaining about the world to each other—something we can never do with Trudy herself as she is too goddamn Zen! It's so fun. Jen and Trudy have this amazing relationship—it's so good that it used to make me sick. IT WAS SO GROSS! They even held hands in the car. GET A FUCKING ROOM! I don't want to see that. For someone as heartily committed to aloneness as I was, it was sometimes hard to take.

I have known them both now for fifteen years, and in that time we have even holidayed together, which is the ultimate test of friendship in my book. They are also the only people whose house I can stay at and feel comfortable. Trudy and Jen have forced me to do things I would never usually do. Nothing too drastic or major, just things like getting outdoors and experiencing life outside of my apartment. Also, they made me buy a cow. I own a cow. WHY DO I OWN A COW? I don't know. Except that Trudy and Jen made me do it. The cow isn't even to eat. It's a show cow and I will show her at the Ekka (a large Brisbane cattle show), so do stay tuned for that!

Over our years of friendship, I have seen firsthand how wise and incredible Trudy is as a person and she is someone who has taught me a lot about how to handle other relation-ships in my life. The main thing she has shown me is to approach every difficult situation by putting myself in the other person's shoes. She has made me realise the world doesn't revolve around me (as much as I want it to). Everyone is different, and not everything comes from a place of selfishness and the desire to just be right. When someone disagrees with you, it's not because they hate you—it's probably because they have had a totally different upbringing and have developed completely different views due to the path their life has taken them on. She is such a kind person. I want to be like her—I really do!—but deep down, I just hate other people and, as hard as I try, I'm still super intolerant and impatient. But at least I try now—in that way, she has definitely made me a better person.

There are just some friends who have a profound impact on your life, and Trudy is one of them for me. I would hate to think how much of a little bitch I would be if we had never met that year at summer camp. I am honestly so lucky to have found the friends I have. I don't know why I struggle to make connections or why I don't have the desire to or enjoy making connections with more people on a deeper level. It's just not who I am, I guess. I don't need a lot of close friends, but I have found the people I do need, and they are Trudy, Jen and Ashleigh. They are all fucking lesbians, too, so I can't even talk about hot guys with them.

And here is one last fun fact about my closest friends: Trudy's vagina is the only vagina I have seen in real life. It was during a break from summer camp one year when all the counsellors hired a huge mansion together. It was like a classic frat party: bad music, red cups and everyone except me heinously drunk. I went to bed early, on the floor in the corner away from all the action, just hoping to wake up the next morning to the party being over. Picture me rocking back and forth whispering to myself, 'This will all be over soon.'

I finally got to sleep among all the noise only to be woken up by Trudy, who was standing over me, completely nude holding a half-empty glass of tequila. HER VAGINA WAS IN MY FACE! I was under her vagina looking right up into it. She then drunkenly said sorry and ran away.

It was at that moment that I became ten per cent gayer than I already was. I was a gay. Definitely a gay. But I still love my three girls.

Part Two

LEAVING THE HOUSE

6

THE SAFETY OF INDOORS

I am and always have been an indoor kind of person. I love living alone and just watching TV and chilling inside in the safety of my soft and comfy couch.

My favourite thing to do when I was a kid was whinge and complain. My second favourite thing was to collect the scrap pieces of wood Dad would discard in his shed and bang nails into them. I would sit by myself in our big backyard just going at it, and all you could hear was the thud of the hammer missing the nail and the block of wood every time and just hitting the pavers. If you were to look at those pavers now, you would still be able to see the broken ones. I did that, with my manly strength.

Mum and Dad were always more of your outdoor-type parents. Holidays to the South Coast of New South Wales and winter trips to the Blue Mountains. Constant hiking and adventuring. They wanted us to explore the outdoors as much as possible. I appreciate what they were trying to do, however, my happy place was when we would return home, through the door and back inside.

That doesn't mean I do not have a deep and profound appreciation of the beauty of nature—I do, just from inside the comfort of my home. From a safe distance. And if any part of nature happens to come inside this safe zone I become a nervous wreck, a ball of tears, and can only sleep again once the offending nature has been eradicated or removed from my apartment.

Let me give you an example. Moths! They are like kamikaze killing machines. They look horrible, are powdery and huge and they have the most unpredictable flight path—you think you are getting out of their way when suddenly they fly into your mouth. Moths are the single most horrifying creatures on god's great Earth. Give me a spider over a moth any day.

The main thing that makes moths total freaks within the bug world is that they move on three axes. Spiders only go up and down. Statistics show that a spider is more likely to be hit by a thrown shoe than a moth is. Trying to kill a moth is virtually a mission impossible, with my attempts mostly involving me crying and screaming while waving a tea towel around. I once tried to use fly spray, but it did nothing but cause me to stop breathing and my eyes to sting for hours. My

THE SAFETY OF INDOORS

place smelled horrible for days after and that fucking moth was still alive somewhere in my flat.

The aftermath of a moth attack is like a war zone. All the objects you have thrown at the moth are strewn around the room—paintings have fallen, there are shoe prints on the walls. I once without thinking threw a shoe at a moth that was resting on a glass light fixture and I smashed the light and glass went everywhere and the BLOODY MOTH WAS STILL ALIVE! Another time, I had to spend three nights in my guestroom because I had locked a moth in my bedroom. I HATE MOTHS!

I'm sure it doesn't help that when I was a kid, I was told that if a moth's powder touches you it will kill you. As an adult I know that's not true, but I still get completely freaked out when one touches me.

To make matters worse, when I lived in Adelaide for a few years in my twenties while pursuing a career in radio, I encountered the bogong moth. Wikipedia says that the bogong moth is 'notable for its biannual long-distance seasonal migrations'. BULL-FUCKING-SHIT! It's notable because it is fucking enormous!!! When I say enormous, I mean dinner plate enormous. Before my bogong moth encounter, I thought all moths were created equal. What I didn't realise was that I had actually lived a very sheltered life from moths.

This is how the trauma went down in Adelaide. I was in the hip inner-city suburb of Unley and was walking into the city to get dinner—it was dark and the streetlights were the only source of any light. I was walking up Peacock Road, a heavily tree-lined suburban street that cuts through a park, minding my own business, listening to music. As I walked, I noticed that small pieces of thick bark were regularly falling from the dark trees and onto the path. I remember feeling a piece of bark fall on me and get stuck on my jumper. This piece was about as big as a drink coaster. The bark then proceeded to start walking. That's odd, I thought, and quickly brushed it off. It fell to the ground and I leant over it, trying to make out what it was. I honestly thought it was just a big but very light piece of bark. I stood there staring at it but due to all the shadows of the trees caused by the streetlights, I couldn't make out if it was still moving or if I was drunk. I used the torch on my phone to assist in identifying what this curious bark-like object actually was and as soon as the light hit the dark mass, I let out the loudest scream I have ever expelled from my body, farted and ran like the fucking wind. I had to run past all the trees and my brain was telling me that the bark on these trees was not bark at all but these creatures. I was convinced these trees were just vertical stacks of this winged creature. I had a slight panic attack and couldn't breathe. I started laughing at how funny the situation was, but still felt like I was in a horror movie. Peacock Road is long, and it took me ages to get away from those trees.

What had transpired was that I'd had my first up-close and personal encounter with the bogong moth, or what I say is hands down the biggest, ugliest, most terrifying moth mankind is capable of imagining. It was on my fucking jumper about twenty centimetres from my mouth. I regrouped and treated myself to about nine pizzas and a few doughnuts to recover. I then had to make the hardest decision of my life. Do I walk an extra 400 metres to avoid Peacock Road or go home via the quickest and easiest route—past the Trees of Moth? For someone who is as lazy as me, there was a third option calling my name, so I got into the safety of a taxi. The driver took me literally forty-five seconds down the road and I gave him a tip. He saved my life. I am forever grateful.

Since that fateful night, I have had approximately 600 more encounters with my nemesis, the moth—most of them just as dramatic as the first. If there is a moth in my apartment, it's worse for me than if someone has broken in wielding an axe. You can negotiate with an axe murderer—you can give them what they want: money, your body, whatever. But one cannot bargain with a moth because a moth knows not what it wants. Hence the crazy flying. I have learned to compose myself a little better since a neighbour had to come in and check I was okay during another encounter. It was in the late afternoon and I got home from work and there was a huge moth flying around my living room. Any sane human would see that, relative to human size, the moth was small, but to me all moths are large and scary. I opened all the doors and windows, grabbed a nearby magazine and began to frantically wave it at the moth, desperately and hopelessly trying to shoo it out an open door or window—a futile activity given their erratic flight paths at the best of times. There may have also been loud audible yelps and prolonged shrieking any time the moth came near me and the fact that all the doors and windows were open meant that anyone within a five-kilometre radius could pretty much hear me. They must have either thought I was being attacked or having the weirdest sex of my life. I was screaming and gagging at the same time, while also making loud thumping noises as I swiped at items and surfaces. One of my neighbours—who I had never spoken to before and never spoke to again after-wards—decided that she would pop her head in to just make sure I wasn't being stabbed and stuffed into barrels (this was in Adelaide, after all). She politely knocked on the open front door and asked if I was okay. Out of total fear and embarrass-ment, I just let out a really loud forced laugh and said everything was fine. IT ABSOLUTLEY WASN'T! I was filled with shame and made up a lie about how a bird had got in my apartment. She laughed too and I told her the bird had just gone, that she had just missed it, it had flown out a window. She said goodbye and left, giving me a slightly suspicious look as she did so. The twist: she must have somehow taken the moth with her as she left, as after the door closed behind her I couldn't find it anywhere. It had vanished. I collapsed onto the couch and just lay there, catching my breath through sobs. My only solace was to spend the next ninety minutes on Grindr and console myself with dick pics. Grindr saves lives.

It wasn't until I bought my handheld Dyson vacuum that I truly felt safe. After that, when a moth was found inside, I would grab the Dyson and it was like a scene from *Ghostbusters*. Attach brush nozzle. Activate moth-catching device. Pull trigger and point in the direction of the moth. The arm of the Dyson was long and the vacuum was light, so it was like a little moth gun. Just wave the Dyson around frantically on full suction power—it always worked. My Dyson is like my child, it's literally the only thing I would grab in a fire.

Looking back now, I think my general disdain of outdoor activities started quite young. When I was growing up my family lived near the Ryde Aquatic Leisure Centre, and Mum enrolled us in swimming lessons there, which we would go to every Saturday morning. It was the most amazing aquatic centre ever: there was not just one but NINE POOLS! A heated pool that felt like you were swimming in piss (which you probably were), the 'T' pool, shaped like the letter T (where I did all my swimming lessons) and then the worst of all the pools— the diving pool, complete with a 650-metre diving platform (I was just a kid so forgive me if my measurements are slightly off). This diving pool was the deepest body of water I had ever seen. What was particularly horrifying was the fact that due to some overzealous chlorination, you could actually see the bottom of the pool—and it was about eight kilometres away.

'Okay, class, jump in and swim across to the other side,' my swimming instructor said one innocent day that was about to turn into my worst nightmare. I was about eight years old and had just done a full lesson in the T pool, and now we were being asked to jump into the diving pool and then swim across the deepest body of water in the history of aquatic centres for a diving lesson. Get stuffed, there was no way. As a kid, when I didn't want to do something I would generally just cry, and nine times out of ten it worked. Ah, how I long now for those simpler times. However, that day, surrounded by my whole class and at the impressionable age of eight, I couldn't bring myself to turn on the waterworks and reveal myself to be the massive wimp I knew I was. So I got in and immediately pissed myself—as in, actually urinated due to fear. My breathing got heavy and I started thrashing about, like I was drowning.

'Christian, are you okay?' I heard yelled across the entire pool.

No, you stupid idiot, clearly I was not—I was hyperventilating and about to shit myself from the sheer terror that I was in the deepest water I had ever been in. I honestly thought sharks lived in any water deeper than Nan and Pa's pool.

In true Christian fashion, I was the last one to reach the other side (I can't lie, that wasn't an altogether unfamiliar experience for me). Getting to the other side was a massive achievement for me and I was just so proud and elated that I bloody did it. While I was busy high-fiving myself, in the background I heard my swimming instructor call out, 'Back you come, Christian!'

Get fucked, you witch!

Instead, I got out of the pool and just walked back. When she asked why I hadn't swum back, I thought I was very clever by replying, 'Oh sorry, you didn't specify.'

After the class was told to line up to dive into the pool from the springboard, I pulled her aside and told her I was too scared. She was actually lovely about it and said it was okay. Mainly because I was the cutest kid and would put on a show of charm when trying to get out of something.

That was the last time I ever went into the diving pool.

Another fateful day that springs to mind from when I was a little human turd, maybe about nine years old, is a day that Mum took me and the triplets (then four years old) to a nearby park with an awesome bike track. She was on her own with four rambunctious boys running in all different directions.

I loved this park as it was like a small taste of independence. I would jump on my bike and ride along the cycle path, which weaved around little hills and trees and snaked in and out of shadows. There was one section in particular that made me feel so free—it was out of sight of Mum and she couldn't see me when I rode. I loved that. Off in my own world, with no one watching over my shoulder. This was how I came to have some appreciation of the outdoors—the catch was, I had to be alone. I love being alone at the beach or on a hike. I honestly cannot stand being with anyone when I go for walks.

These days when I visit my parents (who now live in the Blue Mountains), I often want to take a walk on my own for some quiet time out. But the moment I mention that I am about to head out, Dad will jump in with, 'I'll join you!' I hate this so much. I usually go for walks to be alone and just be at one with my thoughts. I can't do that if Dad's there, yapping away. I am such an ungrateful son. Just so you know that I am not a total jerk, I should add that we do sometimes go on walks together, Mum included, and they are lovely, but sometimes I just need to be alone.

Anyway, back to being nine at the bike park and the sweet, sweet exhilaration of having two minutes of unsupervised riding. So, Mum had let us all go off on our bikes, and was watching us from afar. We were playing with the other kids there, having the time of our lives. Suddenly, I look over and see that Mum is trying to round up my brothers, in order for us to head home. Imagine a woman trying to get three blowflies into a jar. That's what it was like for Mum with the triplets. Impossible. She would get the hand of one and then reach for another, only to have the one she was holding break free and run. God even knows where the third one was by then.

While this was going on, I decided in my pea-brained wisdom that it would be hilarious to hide from her. Yes, hide, in a park, as a young child. So I did and then I watched her have a huge freak-out when she couldn't find me. I thought it was so funny. Obviously, now as an adult, I realise it's an awful thing to do and I still constantly apologise to Mum for it, but at that time when I was nine, it was all a big game and I loved it. After about twenty minutes had gone by, I decided the time was right to spring out and yell, 'Boo!'

The level of calm my mother had when she realised I had been hiding from her the whole time was huge. She didn't yell or scream. She simply bundled us into the car, got into the driver's seat and drove us home in silence. Her face was white and she was expressionless. Turns out this wasn't because she was chill—it was the calm before the storm, masking murderous rage, the kind of rage you get right before you brutally kill someone. You *appear* to be calm, but your insides are on fire. She wasn't thrilled that day, but as I always say, this was her burden to bear—she chose to have kids, so she had to reap the rewards.

We were always taken to parks to expel our energy as kids. It wasn't the worst strategy in the world for parents of four boys. There were heaps of great parks in our area and there was one at Meadowbank that was particularly big and a favourite. It was at this Meadowbank park that I did something subconsciously that is so Christian—and also so inappropriate.

The four of us were with Mum and some of the neighbourhood kids and their parents. We were sitting in one of the fields close to some play equipment when one of the neighbourhood kids ran up and proclaimed: 'That man showed me his penis!' It turns out there was a man in a trench coat in the play area, flashing the children. I was about eleven and I remember being super curious and wanting to have a look. So I stood up and announced to the group: 'I wanna see his penis too!'—a line I still use to this day.

I remember Mum shouting at me to sit down while she went to the car to call the police. Mobile phones weren't a thing yet, but we had a car phone. (Something I was proud of because only rich people had car phones—I even took it to school for show and tell one year.)

While Mum was off calling the police, I desperately tried to find this man. I asked the kid where they'd seen him and I tried to sneak away from the group to find him. Alas, I did not. But every time I went to that park from that day on, I had my eyes peeled for Penis Man—if I got a second chance, I was going to be ready.

My philosophy here is simple: if there is dick to be seen, I'll go outside. But if there isn't, then it's unlikely I will want to venture into nature or the sun.

In my teen years, my hermit-like tendencies really blossomed—I really retreated to my room. It wasn't good enough to just be indoors, I also needed to be shut in my room, alone.

I decided to live in my room and only come out for meals or to grunt at my parents on the day that I found a TV out the front of some random house during a local council clean-up. I brought it home without permission and set it up in my room.

Just to give you an idea of how indulged I was as a kid, my room was actually the master bedroom of the house—it was huge and had a desk that Dad had made that went wall to wall, like a big workbench. I had been given a boom box (for those of you under thirty, this is a portable stereo/radio) that was on the desk, and I would sit there to do my homework or art projects while listening to the Hot30 or Ugly Phil. My art projects mostly involved making things out of wire and making jewellery. I was always creating.

You have to remember that back then there were no iPhones or iPads, no TikTok, not even a desktop computer with the internet. All I had was my desk, the boom box, some art supplies and a TV. But I was happy! I loved being in my own little world, listening to music and making things. It's funny, really, because now I both live alone and am always making things. Nothing has changed.

It wasn't until my later teen years that things went a little weird. I knew I was different. I knew I was gay. But I was awkward and I didn't want to talk to my parents about things, so I just sat in my room and watched TV. My room was a sanctuary where I did not have to deal with anything. I could just create random little sculptures, listen to music and chill: still my ideal way to spend an evening!

I've never really been a party person either—as a teen and still as an adult. I just don't really get the appeal. I don't drink alcohol and never really have, I don't do illicit drugs or get high and most of all I don't enjoy party games and socialising en masse. Parties just don't do it for me. The loud music, the people screeching and squealing, the stupid dancing, the boring repetitive drunk conversations, spilt drinks, trashed houses, projectile vomiting: it is a hard no from me. If I *must* spend time with other people, I prefer to just hang out with one or two close friends at the most.

Another thing I hate about parties is balloons. They scare the living shit out of me. I don't know why I have this morbid fear of them. I can only assume that something bad and balloon related must have happened to me when I was a kid. I think this is how it would have gone...

Young Christian gets given a bright and gorgeous balloon one day and is just loving himself—holding it, bobbing it up and down without a care in the world, living his best life and feeling extremely happy. He is at peace, he is calm, he is one with the world. Then—when he least expects it and just when he has dropped his guard and really started *living*—BANG!! His beloved balloon loudly explodes in his face and scares the living shit out of him. He cries and cries (he may have pooed his pants a little bit), and from that day forward Christian never trusts a balloon again.

I do have a vague memory of being about eight years old and blowing up a balloon so much—too much—that it exploded in my face. So, that's at least one balloon trauma that I *do* recall—I can only imagine how many more I have repressed.

Balloons are not fun—they never have been. They are loud bangs waiting to happen. They are just horrible things that cause mass anxiety. I DON'T GET THEM. Why? Who the hell thought up this concept of a party accessory that could turn evil at the slightest wrong touch? And what the hell was wrong with them? Who thinks: I want to make a toy that can explode loudly at any time without warning?

And why the hell are they marketed at children? I suspect that whoever invented balloons secretly hated children. And secretly hated all people. And secretly hated life. And that's why we have balloons. It is the only explanation that makes any sense.

Because aren't streamers enough? Why go so overboard on decorations? Just use fucking streamers and those expanding crepe-paper objects—they're fab and are highly unlikely to trigger a heart attack for Uncle Kevin at little Timmy's fourth birthday party by going off like a fucking gunshot in the middle of musical chairs. Why put everyone on edge the entire duration of a party by having FUCKING BALLOONS?! I hate them so much.

Is their sole purpose to teach kids about distrust? Have this fun-looking thing, how pretty are the colours, put all your trust in this balloon, little Timmy, then BANG! It's gone, all your hopes and dreams explode with the balloon, it scares you and makes you instantly sad and then you cry. You loved that balloon and now it is gone, without any explanation as to why. LIFE ISN'T FAIR, LITTLE TIMMY!

But by far the worst type of balloon is a rogue balloon in the office. There's nothing worse than a balloon in an adults-only environment. We startle more easily, with more serious consequences than children. Look around the office: can you see any children? Is little Timmy sitting somewhere in a quiet corner? No? Well, then there is no fucking call for balloons. Ever.

Except . . . sometimes you will find them there, far from their natural habitat. Why, you ask? It's because some careless individual thought it would be a great idea to fill the space around Kaycee's desk with balloons because it's her birthday.

Kaycee doesn't want these fucking dumb balloons—first, she can't get to her computer, and then she has to clean up the stupid mess that you thought was a lovely gesture, but it's not, Tina, it's a fucking waste of time and now I am super anxious about all the balloons just bouncing around the office. We all *know* office carpet is full of staples that are tangled in the fibres. One wrong move on the carpet and BANG! Everyone jumps, but not me—no, I screech so fucking loudly, then I cry, then I realise I've pissed my pants.

And even then, after all that, there are still nine more goddamn balloons lolling around the floor. No one seems to ever take responsibility for them, so they remain on the floor till they all explode, one by heart attack–inducing one. Then, once they have all exploded and at long last your extreme anxiety is given a break from the perils of this rainbow-coloured literal MINEFIELD, some other fucker has a birthday and the entire process starts again. Argggghhhhhh!

Balloons: I can't be anywhere near them. If there is a party with balloons, here is my advance RSVP right now: no fucking way will I be coming. And this will continue to be my policy until the human race wakes up to its extreme stupidity in embracing these death-baits and makes them illegal. The criminalisation of balloons and the subsequent balloon crimes tribunals will be my gift to the world, my legacy. You are welcome.

7

ON THE ROAD

Another reason for my major objection to leaving the house (unless I absolutely have to) is the actual act of getting from A to B. I do NOT love 'public transport'. Mostly because I do not love the 'public'.

Have you ever noticed that one of the most annoying parts of public transport is the stupidity of the old people who catch it? Take note, older readers: if I offer you my seat on any mode of public transport, sit your old ass down, take the goddamn seat. I'm getting up because I clearly think you need it.

I get so frustrated when a proud old biddy gets on the tram only to refuse an offered seat because she thinks she is fine to stand. She is too proud to admit she has aged horribly, her bones have brittled and her muscles are weak. Sit in the seat, you old bitch.

I can't sit back in the seat I've just vacated because then I look like an inconsiderate young person who is a selfish asshole. Yes, I absolutely am a selfish asshole, but I don't want other people to think that. Which is why I offer the elderly my seat. But time and time again, these stupid selfish oldies say no. And when that happens?

Well, now we are both standing and there is a vacant seat. Good work, Bev, really good work. I hope you are proud of yourself.

Needless to say, the very day I turned sixteen, I took my first step to transportational independence and got my learner driver's licence. I think at the time I believed that the moment I was *enlicensed*, my life would be transformed into the kind of luxury lifestyle of the rich and famous that Ashleigh and I fantasised about (and knew we both deserved) in maths class when we should have been learning trigonometry (seriously, no regrets there).

The reality, however, of getting my licence was—hmm, how do I put it?—completely fucking mental. The key to this process being such a clusterfuck was the terrible idea that my mum should teach me how to drive.

So, when Mum would take me out for a driving lesson, she was the worst, most nervous teacher you could ever imagine. She spent the entire time we were in the car shouting and yelling uncontrollably—and not even constructively, instead about almost nothing. She would loudly proclaim that there was a red light ahead, however, at that stage the set of lights would still be ten kilometres away, and by the time I got to them they would always be green. Alternatively, she would tell me that the lights *after* the next set of lights were red and then she would grip the side of her seat and the door handle, white-knuckle style, like she was in a plane that was heading straight for the ground. This was Mum's go-to move. She knew the yelling and screaming wasn't helpful so instead she would grip the seat so tightly that she even ripped the fabric at one point. She would do this no matter what I did. Mum's fucked-up equations for teaching me to drive included:

- Slight acceleration = Tightly gripping the seat
- Braking = High-pitched noises + tightly gripping the seat
- Going into reverse = Looking frantically in every direction + tightly gripping the seat
- Turning on the ignition while in the driveway = Hyper-ventilating into a bag + tightly gripping the seat
- Me asking her to take me driving = Desperately hoping Dad was around to do it instead + tightly gripping the walls.

This horror show didn't last long, as I quickly learned that I hated driving with Mum as it made me feel like I was a terrible driver and we would both end up screaming at each other. On the other hand, Dad was an actual saint at teaching me to drive. I don't get how a man who would lose his mind at the smallest thing, like the dishwasher being stacked incorrectly or the fact he couldn't find the pepper in the cupboard, could be so damn calm when death was staring him in the face. I admit that driving with me was literally like asking yourself, 'Is today the day? Will Christian kill us all today?'

In the end, Mum and Dad ended up paying someone else to give me lessons—I needed a professional it seems. Their decision in reality was probably due to the fact that they wanted to maintain good familial relationships with each other and with me and they knew that if either of them continued to teach me to drive, it would either end up in a divorce or me applying for parental emancipation or both.

Finally, FINALLY, I got my licence. Let's just say I got it first go. (Book fact-checker, put that red pen down NOW, just move right along please!) I thought it was the end of my transport troubles but really they'd only just begun. The best way I can explain what kind of driver I am is by saying: I take after my mother.

I turn into the Hulk when I drive. I don't know why I'm so intolerant of everyone on the road. Every little thing sets me off. For example, things that drive me fucking crazy on the road include:

- If I'm behind someone going slow
- If someone is tailgating me when I'm going THE SPEED LIMIT
- Getting stuck behind someone turning right and holding up the whole lane
- Literally anyone on the road, doing anything.

I don't just get angry—I say things that could get me arrested. One time I got so mad while at a set of lights that I loudly said the C-bomb a few times and wondered why some pedestrians suddenly turned to look at me. I had the window down.

I would never toot the horn at someone though. For some reason, I just can't bring myself to do it and I don't know why. My first car was a Volvo—this was my dad's decision. He wanted me to be inside the car that most resembled an army tank. He found a second-hand champagne-coloured Volvo and he bought it for me. I think it was from the 1980s and it was the most solid, brick-like car I had ever seen. I can tell you that this car was actually worth it. The number of walls and poles I hit was in the high forties and the car never got a dent. The walls I hit would literally crumble and the sound when I hit them was horrible, but when I would get out to inspect the damage, there never was any. This may have made me a little careless, I guess, as when parking, I would often only know that I had reversed all the way in when the wall would tell me. It generally went like this:

Me: Reverse. Reverse. Twiddle with radio. Glance at mirror. Reverse. Take bite of the McDonald's cheeseburger in my hand.

Wall: BANG!

Me: Stop. Move slightly forward. Exit vehicle. Finish cheeseburger.

When the Volvo died, I was given my grandfather's little red Nissan Pulsar. I had that for a few years and didn't have any accidents or issues. I felt so cool driving that car. It was small and zippy and a bit like a really cool person's car. It was from the early nineties.

But one year after I had been working as a camp counsellor over in the States, I returned to find that the little red Nissan had been replaced by a green one. It was a newer model and looked like the kind of car your average Joe would drive. I no longer felt cool driving. Even though I was the most uncool person, that red Nissan had given me the kind of hot-guy confidence/arrogance that I needed. I could not believe I had been blindsided by my father like this. To be fair, I had never actually paid for or owned any of these cars, so I wasn't really allowed to be angry.

From Dad's perspective, I returned home from three months in the States and, *wow*, I had a new car. It was newer, it had a CD player and it was just better than my old car. However, I needed time to grieve my red Nissan and I never had the chance to do that. I'm not joking—that red Nissan was like a close friend. We did everything together, Macca's Drive Thru breakfast, Macca's Drive Thru lunch and then Macca's Drive Thru dinner. Also, I was still a virgin when I owned the red Nissan. The plan was to be inside a safe space (my Nissan) while someone ventured into my safe space for the first time. So much for that. I no longer had that safe space. It was going to be a while before any car sex was to take place.

To add insult to injury, as he threw me the keys (after I had finished weeping and wailing), Dad added: 'By the way, mate, the new car is a manual.'

For fuck's sake, Dad.

I was already a shit driver and now he'd gone and made driving even more difficult for me. I'd learned on an automatic—in fact, I hadn't even quite mastered how to drive an auto and now Dad had gone and got me a manual car. Not to sound ungrateful, but FUCK, Dad, why?!

Our neighbours at the time owned a farm and we had sometimes gone on family trips out to their farm at Bathurst during the school holidays, where we'd get on the quad bikes and be hoons. We would also take their cars for a drive around the paddocks. The cars were manual, and Dad would happily instruct us how to drive them. So, to be fair to Dad, I did have a basic knowledge of how to drive a manual car.

NOT ON THE ROAD, IN A PADDOCK.

A paddock has zero objects to hit. You are in a field of nothing. In the real world, it's vastly different. But Dad just told me I would be fine and to have a great first day back at work. 'I'm not driving myself to work in that,' I declared. After my outburst, Dad decided that it was wise for him to accompany me for the first drive and, my god, was it hysterical.

I literally bunny hopped all the way to work. A ten-minute drive took about forty-five minutes. It was funny and then frustrating and then really funny and then stressful as cars behind me just thought I was the biggest idiot. I couldn't even hide behind L-plates—I had my full licence. It took about three days for me to get the hang of it and then I was off on my own, feeling like the smartest person in the world. I felt so cool and at every possible opportunity would find myself casually dropping into conversation that I could drive a manual car. EVERY CONVERSATION.

Imagine a scenario where I am meeting a new work colleague. This is how it would generally go:

Me: Hi, I'm Christian. If you need any help on the till, let me know. There is also an issue with the printer that we need to sort, so don't worry about the labels for today. I'm going to go to Officeworks on my way home and get a new one for us. I'll need to take my car to do that. It's a manual. Which means obviously I'm better than you.

New work colleague: I drive a manual too.

Me: Let's spend the next fifteen minutes loudly discussing how superior we are to everyone because we can drive a manual. My favourite thing to do is change from second gear into third—it gives me a real rush!

New work colleague: Should I help this customer?

After driving my MANUAL car for a few years, I had my first accident (not my fault). I cannot stress enough how much it wasn't my fault. It was on Victoria Road in Sydney, near the intersection of Darling Street in Rozelle. I was heading into the city and the road goes up a slight hill. It has three lanes of usually busy traffic and at the top of the hill is a set of lights. I was travelling the speed limit in the middle lane and the traffic in both lanes either side of me was going fast. Suddenly, for no apparent reason, my lane wasn't moving, and it took me by surprise. I slammed on the brakes and by a hair stopped short of hitting the car in front of me. I looked in my rear-vision mirror to see if the car behind me had clocked the scene. The following happened in the space of three seconds and it's the quickest my brain has ever worked. In the mirror, I noticed a motorbike swerving in and out of the lanes and registered that the car behind me was going quite fast. I realised that the driver of the car was going to be concentrating on not hitting the motorbike and therefore would not realise the middle lane had come to a stop. I knew in that moment that the car was going to hit me—and hard. I didn't want to then slam into the car in front of me, so I took my foot off the brake and rolled back a bit and then put my foot as hard as I could on the brake.

The impact was horrifying and sickening and I didn't know what to do. The traffic was still zooming past us, and there was no way we could get out of our vehicles where we were, so I gingerly changed lanes and pulled into the nearest spot on Darling Street, the other car pulling up behind me shortly afterwards. I was so scared that this guy was going to be fuming. I noticed it was an Audi and a good one. I sat in my car and waited and waited. He wasn't getting out either. I decided to open my door and fumble around to make it look like I was getting out and then I was hoping he would too. I was convinced he was going to stay in his car and abuse me and that I'd cry.

As I did my mock exit performance, he literally did everything that I was doing at the same time. I opened my door, he opened his door, I put one foot out, he put one foot out. It was like we were doing the hokey-pokey. I stood up and then so did he. He was an older man and looked timid. But once he saw how short and unintimidating I was, he walked over to me.

It turned out that he was a lovely guy who had sadly been involved in a previous accident with a man who had tried to hurt him, so he was understandably terrified. But when he'd seen me, he obviously thought I was so weak-looking that he could easily outrun me if he needed to. He was absolutely correct. Thankfully, no running was required that day for either of us, which was a relief as the day was traumatic enough as it was.

We exchanged details and it was the smoothest, easiest insurance claim I think I'll ever have to deal with. His insurance company was so elite and exclusive they wanted nothing to do with my shitty car and paid me out the value. It was basically written off due to the cost of replacing almost every panel on the car. It was a $7000 job, so they gave me $4500 for the car. And I kept the money *and* the car. WHAT A WIN! Dad had been the one to buy me the car (he paid $4000) but I was the one getting to keep the money. Entrepreneurial or what!

Here is where things get a bit dodgy. The only real problem was the boot. After the accident, I needed to duct tape it down as it wouldn't close. Mechanically, everything was totally fine. But there was so much duct tape holding everything down and on and together. I drove that patchwork car for about three more years.

In New South Wales, to get the roadworthy certificate needed for registration, you just need your local mechanic to sign off on it. I would take the car to my wonderful mechanic, get that certificate from them, thank them for being legends, register the car for another year and drive the car around, boot strapped on with tape. To be fair, it was totally roadworthy, if that road had very low standards.

My luck ran out when I moved to Adelaide for a job. My rego was up and I needed to renew it. I thought I'd just do the same thing I'd been doing for three years—the car was fine and it would be fine to register. Sadly, in South Australia, the laws are slightly different and I was mortified when I found out how.

In order to register my vehicle, I had to go to the motor registry—there was no option to handpick my own corruptible dodgy mechanic. When I got there, I drove down a driveway past a long queue of people all waiting to get their car rego. In my mind, I was just going to park my car in the carpark, go in to get my sticker and then leave. So I'm driving past all these eyes, staring at me as I cruise down the long driveway. At that precise moment, my car decided to make the noise of a dying cat—a sound it had never made before, mind you. This loud high-pitched screech drew a lot of attention to me and this sound wasn't coming from my mouth (for a change). It was at this point that everyone but me knew there was no way I was driving out of that place with my rego.

The noise was hideous and embarrassing. Initially my window had been down as I'd puttered down the driveway past the sea of judging and—let's call a spade a spade here—schadenfreude-spiked facial expressions. I decided I would wind my window up in an attempt to maintain a shred of anonymity—and an even smaller shred of dignity. As I wound the window up as subtly as I could, I kid you not, the knob came off in my hand. Now, I was no stranger to knobs coming off in my hand, but not without at least a little foreplay. I abandoned the window and parked the car out the back. By this stage, I was pretty sure I would still get my car registered. I would just go in and say hi and get the stamp and leave.

Fool of a man!

What I hadn't realised was that they do an inspection of the vehicle, obviously. When my number was called, I handed in my form and was then told to bring my car around for an inspection. As it happens, the inspection was to take place in front of about twenty-five other people, waiting their turn.

So, I brought my loud car around and as I pulled into the big shed where the inspection would happen, all twenty-five faces began to light up. They knew what was coming and they couldn't wait. I'm sure they thought it was their half-time entertainment. A planned comedy bit for them to enjoy, because what kind of massive fuckwit would think that this car covered in duct tape and making the most horrific noise would ever pass a roadworthy test?

Just picture Onslow from *Keeping Up Appearances* pulling up!

I was so mortified. I approached the guy and, still behind the wheel with my window half-up, tried to give him my most innocent and optimistic smile. He asked me if I was going to get the crater-sized chasm in the back of my car fixed. I said no and then he laughed and said there was absolutely no way he would approve my car for registration. He popped a sticker on the windscreen and said I was allowed to drive home and then never drive it again. I was so embarrassed I just agreed and drove off and then cried all the way home.

How was I going to get to my Grindr hook-ups now? Luckily, I lived next door to where I worked, so I really didn't need the car. It was mostly just a mode of transport for my sexcapades. I tried to sell it for $200 and was haggled down to $100.

I was the most confident person on the road and I never thought I would give up driving. But for the next seven years, it didn't worry me to not have a car. My Grindr hook-ups came to me, as well as on me. THIS WAS LIVING!

I can tell you that after seven years with no vehicle, I recently took the plunge and got myself a Mazda. Top of the line, all the unnecessary extras. Sunroof: WTF is that even for? Heated seats: I live in Queensland, literally the sunshine state. Best of all, it's a black car with white leather interiors. I AM SO BOUGIE!

8

BRACING FOR IMPACT

Even the most dedicated homebody would probably admit that going on holidays is maybe one good reason to leave the house. My own history with holiday-making is a little chequered: there have been highs and there have been lows. Holidaying with my family was an awesome part of growing up for me, but it would be a stretch to say that as an adult I have 'wanderlust'. It would be more accurate to say that I have 'couchlust'.

There are people who simply LIVE for travel: their lives are a never-ending cycle of saving for trips, planning trips, talking incessantly about those planned trips, finally eventually taking the damn trip, and then talking incessantly about the trip afterwards. And then the cycle begins again. And sprinkle this vicious cycle with 10,000 Instagram posts of exotic destinations accompanied by far too many annoying hashtags. Jules (my former boss), if you are reading this, I am absolutely talking about you!

To be honest, I find this obsession with travel all a bit exhausting. I often wonder how shit these people's day-to-day lives are that they are constantly obsessed with escaping. (In the case of Jules, I know how shit it was and completely understand why she had to leave the country every three months to cope.) And while I like to see new places and take a break from work, I also really love my daily life—my apartment, my indoor plants, my work and social media and my stashes of Caramilk and KitKat Gold.

When I was a kid, every year we would go on a family holiday—sometimes we'd go twice a year. I don't want you to think we were rich (even though we had a car phone): Mum and Dad didn't get handed money, they worked so hard and sacrificed a lot so we could have the best.

I loved our family holidays. The first one was a trip to Fiji. I was about nine and the triplets were five. It was our first and last time on a plane as a family. To this day, I think it was the most ambitious thing my parents ever did. Who in their right mind would take four boys under the age of ten on a plane to Fiji?

I remember this holiday like it was yesterday. It was the first time I saw someone drunk—a girl who was so unbelievably drunk that she fell down the two flights of stairs just outside our hotel door and her boobs fell out of her top. At the time, I was terrified not only by her boobs but because I thought she was being murdered.

I also remember having a total crush on a boy, like a confusing crush. He was a year younger than me (cradle robber) and looked a little like Matthew Lawrence, who played the eldest son in *Mrs Doubtfire*. He had that nineties haircut and vibe to him. This was a confusing crush because I had friends who were boys, but none who I had ever wanted to make out with. I don't even remember his name. I have learned over the years that names are not important to me. Of all the Grindr hook-ups I have had, I think I can name three of them. I'm a skip-the-formalities-and-just-get-your-top-off kinda guy. However, as a child in Fiji, I wasn't quite the whore I am today. I also think my crush was related to the fact I only ever saw this boy when we were at the pool or beach and he was in speedos.

Fiji was eye-opening for my parents as well as for me: they learned that overseas family holidays were awful. After that trip, we never ventured more than a three-hour drive from home.

While you might think a nice trip to Italy or France would be a beautiful thing to do with your young kids, I can tell you a three-hour drive to a place on the coast is just as bloody brilliant.

Every January, Mum and Dad would rent out a house in Jervis Bay on the New South Wales South Coast. For two weeks, we would go swimming and do whatever we wanted.

To top it all off, we always went with Mum's sister Susie and her family.

Susie's kids, our cousins, were twins, Maddy and Liam, and were a few years younger than my brothers. We had the actual best time. Throwing seaweed at each other, fighting, playing Monopoly and spending twenty-three hours of the day in the water.

I would give up everything to go back and do those holidays again. It was the one time of the year that I could truly be myself. School was hard for me and I had to pretend to be someone else to get by. But when I was at Jervis Bay, I was finally able to be exactly who I was—I didn't have to pretend or worry about anything. It was just me and my family.

Occasionally Mum and Dad would let me go for a walk along the beach by myself. Usually, it was after dinner in the evening, just before the sun went down. I spent a lot of time thinking about stuff, good stuff. I think this was crucial alone time for me, in a supportive environment, surrounded by the most supportive people. I'm pretty sure all the adults in my life knew I was gay. I was a pretty flamboyant kid, and I did stand up and shout 'I wanna see his penis too!' at the park that one time. However, I needed to work my gayness out for myself. I have Jervis Bay to thank for many things.

We used to holiday with my cousins a lot. During the winter months, we would often rent a house in the Blue Mountains for a week and do a lot of bushwalking and exploring. This family time was intense—the houses were smaller, the privacy was limited and there was no alone time. Don't get me wrong: I stilled loved these trips, but it was no Jervis Bay.

Jervis Bay and the Blue Mountains were yearly events. As a family we did this for about nine years before we were all too old and had full-time jobs.

It's interesting to note that I love the indoors but I also am someone who likes to explore. My career in radio has taken me to live in Newcastle on the New South Wales north coast, then to Adelaide, then Melbourne and now I live in Brisbane. I have loved each of these cities. Exploring what they have to offer and the selection of men who I will spend four to five minutes with are highlights for me. My friend Jack jokes that the reason I move to a new city all the time is because I have slept with all the gays and need to move on to new hunting grounds. It sounds so aggressive when he says it, but he isn't wrong. My reputation got so bad in each of these cities that I ultimately needed to pack up and leave if I ever wanted sexy time again.

As you know, from when I was nineteen, I went to the States every summer for three years to be a camp counsellor. That was the kind of travel that worked for me at the time: I was getting out there, but I also didn't have to organise anything myself, it was all done for me. It kind of eased me into the whole overseas travel thing. When I was at camp, we would have a few weeks break, so I did get to see a bit more of America than just the camping grounds I was placed at. These breaks usually consisted of a group of counsellors booking a house nearby together to, essentially, go and get drunk in.

Eventually, in 2015, I bit the bullet and planned a European holiday with my brothers and their girlfriends (now wives). When I say planned, I mean my sister-in-law Jenny planned everything. Our itinerary included: getting ripped off in a cab in Paris, almost being mugged in Naples and locking ourselves out of our Airbnb in London.

This trip was a really eye-opening one for my brothers. It was the first time they got to witness the full Cluelessness of Christian Hull. Here is a quick summary of the misadventures I got us into.

While standing in front of the Eiffel Tower, enjoying the spectacular view, I was accosted by some French people wanting me to sign a petition. They shoved a petition in front of me, essentially blocking my view of anything, and they started to go through my pockets, trying to take my stuff. I had no idea what they were doing and was just happy to be doing my bit for social justice by signing the petition to help sick kids get to the top of the tower. Here I was being Mr Nice Guy while I was actually being robbed. Keep in mind: this was the first day of our trip. My brothers were a little way behind me and they came running up and stopped the commotion. I had no idea why they were shooing away these lovely volunteers who just wanted to get the sick kids to the top of the Eiffel Tower. Luckily, in the end they only took my dignity and nothing else. I still wonder about those sick kids, though, and whether they ever made it to the top.

Later in the trip, we were getting ready to catch a train from Naples to Sorrento when a woman approached us. We had all our bags and looked precisely like the idiot tourists we were. As chief idiot, I told her where we wanted to go and she asked to look at our tickets. I went to give them to her. All of our tickets. Which we needed to get to our destination. Again, I was prepared to hand a stranger our tickets. As I reached out to give them to her, my brother stepped in and he grabbed them off her before I let go of them. I was mortified.

Here was this lovely lady trying to help us, and Nick was being a rude prick. After the lady walked off, offended, Nick explained to me what he believed had been about to happen. She was about to take our tickets from me, after which she would have pointed us in the direction of the platform but would have then refused to give us our tickets back unless we handed over a large sum of cash. His suspicions were backed up by some tourists next to us, who told us that this was exactly what had just happened to them.

The third incident was at the airport in Paris, after we had landed. We were lining up to get into a cab and a man in a suit said to me, 'Follow me, please.' I loudly told everyone 'This way!' and next minute, we were in his cab on our way to our hotel. When we got there, he told us it was an AUD$180 fare. WHAT? He would also only accept cash. He wouldn't give us our bags until we paid. CHRISTIAN, NOT AGAIN! I had no choice but to find an ATM, get out the money and pay the See You Next Tuesday!

I'm a shy puppy in a foreign country. I was just scared of everything. The triplets and their gals would often laugh at how terrified of literally everything I was. I personally think my fear was completely justifiable, given that everyone was either stealing from me or ripping me off. Don't get me wrong, though: I adored Europe. It is the most beautiful history-rich place in the world. Rome was the highlight. The buildings and the men. I managed to sneak away and have relations with a few of the locals. Some spoke no English. IT WAS SO HOT!

In Paris, however, I refused to talk to anyone for fear they would get angry. I'd been told that the locals don't take too kindly to tourists, and every time I wanted to order food or ask a question I would whisper it to one of my brothers, who'd have to speak for me. Turns out the locals were super friendly and I had nothing to worry about.

Given my travel timidity, it might surprise you that a few years later, in 2019, I spent fourteen days in New York in a hotel in Midtown Manhattan. It came about because my newest of friends, Lou, invited me on a trip of a lifetime to help with the filming of some segments for her TV show.

I had first met Lou at VidCon Australia a few months prior—VidCon is an online video tech conference for fans, creators and companies. It goes for three days and includes live on-stage performances, panels, interactive experiences, fan and creator meet and greets and heaps more. I had been invited to attend and host some workshops.

I was at VidCon with my good mate Tanya Hennessy. Tanya and Lou had been on a panel together previously, so they knew each other. Tanya and I were getting into the buffet break-fast with a bunch of other creators who were also at VidCon when in walked Lou. Tanya called out to her, before turning to me and saying, 'You'll love this chick—she is right up your alley.' Over comes this little half-Asian woman looking hot in Gorman. She joined us, was super friendly and we clicked instantly over our indoor plants. I told her my fiddle-leaf fig wasn't doing so well and she straightened up and told me to go to Bunnings and get myself a huge fibreglass pot to soak it in.

I was drawn to her confidence, craziness and utter ridicu-lousness, and the following day I did something I almost never ever do: I agreed to grab a coffee and then go shopping with her at the DFO next to the hotel we were staying in. That day, it was like hanging out with the sister I never had. It was a day filled with laughter and Lou spending far too much money at Sass & Bide.

Ever since then we have stayed friends, and even competed in a half-marathon alongside each other at one stage.

So when the opportunity to travel with Lou came up, I jumped at the chance. We had only been friends for eight months, however, it felt like we had grown up together. I can't explain why it feels like this with Lou—we do have some things in common, like Instagram, but I think what it really comes down to is that we have similar personalities and humour. So even though I am not the world's most enthusiastic tourist, it was a no-brainer for me to say yes. I went because she is fun to hang around with and she was paying, but mostly because she is fun to hang around with.

Finally the day came when we were due to fly out. I was excited and nervous. Nervous first and foremost because I hate flying. It was my first long-haul trip in a while, and ninety minutes in and with thirteen hours to go, my back was already cramping, the tipsy high from the complimentary glass of champagne had worn off and I was sitting between two people, one of them being Lou.

Thank god it was an Airbus: it's really the smaller planes, like 737s and anything smaller than that, that worry me. It is just that damn turbulence. Funnily enough, as a kid I loved flying and I was fine. But that all changed when at age nineteen I headed off on my own for my first US summer camp, starting with my first ever solo international flight to the home of Hollywood (and, somewhat less excitingly, the farm camp that was my actual destination), Los Angeles.

After an emotional airport farewell with the fam, I had boarded and we'd taken off. At this stage, I was relaxed— just super excited about getting to LA. An hour into the flight we were served our food and, as I was sitting right up the back, I was the last person to get a meal. By this time, I was ravenous and I just wolfed it down. The old biddy sitting next to me just picked at her lemon chicken and didn't really eat much. She then opened her OJ and proceeded to take some small but annoyingly loud sips.

Suddenly, out of absolutely nowhere, the plane drops from the sky with force. I'm not being dramatic: it was a scary drop, it felt like that moment when you are at the top of a roller-coaster and you suddenly drop.

Trays of food flew into the air and then, within seconds, we shot straight back up again, and all the trays were suspended mid-air for a split second before they crashed back down all over everyone. I was tightly gripping the seat, screaming and with tears streaming down my face when I heard the words no passenger ever wants to hear.

No, not 'BRACE FOR IMPACT'. Worse than that.

The captain came on the PA and calmly said, 'Cabin crew, please take your seats.' WHAT? NO! They never get asked to sit. What was happening? Why were they sitting? I did not approve of this—surely they needed to be activating the anti-turbulence boosters and calling for backup.

The crew sat down and by this point my heart rate was that of a marathon runner who had just run 900 marathons back-to-back. My breathing sounded like I had a punctured lung and I was sweating profusely. There is something utterly terrifying about being literally in a sideways skyscraper travelling 700 kilometres an hour and feeling it drop out of the air. Once sixty seconds had passed, I was able to take note of my surroundings and look for my emergency exit.

That's when I noticed that I was covered in lemon chicken. And OJ. Just absolutely drenched in old mate's food. When I stuck my head into the aisle, I saw a sea of food and cutlery all over the floor. I felt awful for the crew and I calmed down enough to legitimately write a last will and testament leaving my stamp, rock and keyring collections to my most responsible brother at that time, Tim, adding a request that he put the collections into a museum with a dedication to his brother who sadly perished in an horrific aeroplane accident somewhere over the Pacific Ocean.

So, that's when my fear of flying was born.

It was then made worse by the fact that I became obsessed with the TV show *Air Crash Investigations*. That show taught me a lot of things, like that it's best to sit over the wing and that turbulence cannot bring a plane down.

Thankfully, the flight to New York with Lou was nowhere near as eventful. It was uncomfortable, as all flights are, but there was minimal turbulence and the cabin crew remained standing the entire time.

And once we got there, spending two weeks in a city like New York was crazy. It's so unbelievably busy, yet somehow because of how huge it was, I felt quite alone. I literally crammed in so much without feeling like I had really done anything. Occasionally, it did overwhelm me, but luckily Lou is the type of friend who isn't needy, so I was able to take some time out to hide away and be alone every now and then while she filmed some of the show. Even so, we spent heaps of time together and it made me realise how polar opposite we are in the way we travel.

I am the type of tourist who is happy to just go to the touristy places—but Lou is definitely not that type of traveller. This forced me to go to places I had never heard of and they turned out to be the best parts of the trip. Among my highlights were Eataly in Flatiron, which was just wall-to-wall cheese and delicious food, Murray's Cheese in Greenwich Village and Michael Kors in SoHo. I would never have even gone to New York if it weren't for Lou. I struggle to do anything outside my comfort zone and not having a partner means I would basically have to travel alone, and that is way way way out of the comfort zone.

And I have to hand it to Lou, too, as travelling with me would have been the biggest punish of all time. Lou is confident and nothing really bothers her. For example, where I would obsessively abide by the 'walk' and 'don't walk' crosswalk lights, which absolutely no one in New York follows, Lou would just cross the road, while I gasped and screamed at her, or made her wait with me, or just shouted after her, 'I will not accompany you to the hospital when you get run over.' Basically what I am trying to say is that when I'm travelling, I'm timid and a real stickler for the rules and Lou gives no fucks about the rules.

Another difference in our approaches was that I never wanted to cause a scene or a fuss and would always only talk soberly and seriously to any locals for fear of accidentally offending them with my Aussie slang. NOT LOU! She would get right in there with her inaudible Aussie accent and her crazy fucking Aussie slang and ask a million little questions. Half the time, the people she was jabbering on to had no idea what she was saying, but this would only make her more determined and she would end up just repeating herself 1000 decibels louder while I stood in the background, either apologising in what by that stage would almost be a British accent and/or pretending we weren't together. This never worked. For either of us.

One day, I was excited to go with her to the American Museum of Natural History where the movie *Night at the Museum* had been filmed. We got to the museum and I was buying the tickets when the lady serving me asked if we were sure this was the museum we wanted. I thought to myself, 'Yes, this is a museum, and this was the address of the right one!' I politely answered yes and went to pay for the tickets when Lou interrupted and asked, 'Is there a spot where all the things from the movie are? Like just one room?'

First, stupid question. The movie was filmed in the entire museum and they haven't now put all the exhibits in one room to make it easy for tourists. Second, I swear to god, I thought Lou was going to then ask a follow-up question of whether the exhibits actually came to life at night. She denies it, but to this day, I guarantee that she was in fact about to ask that question, but thankfully the lady behind the counter spoke first, and told us we had the wrong museum and we should have been next door.

This was the moment I realised Lou's annoying questions were actually super useful. I would have just paid the US$65 and wandered around some random museum thinking that the movie lied to us.

Turns out the *Night at the Museum* museum next door was about twenty times bigger than the one we'd been about to buy tickets for. Some might even say that it was impossible to miss but fuck those jerks.

Another example of Lou giving zero fucks about the rules was when, while on our trip, she arranged an interview with Mark Manson—the author of the international bestselling books *The Subtle Art Of Not Giving A F*ck* and *Everything is F*cked* (his asterisks, not mine), which are both books that speak to me. Lou met Mark on one of her typically insane opportunities—exactly the kind of thing that could only ever happen to Lou. She was offered an interview with Sir Richard Branson on his private island in the British Virgin Islands. She took the trip, which is where she met Mark, who was a guest speaker, and they struck up a little friendship.

So seeing we were in Mark's small hometown of NYC filming a show, Lou got in touch and asked him if he was free for a chat. He said yes, and we met up with him and filmed an interview with him in Central Park. He was a lovely guy and did the interview like a total pro, then signed some books for us and went on his merry way. It was such a bizarre experience being in New York and just casually chatting with one of the hottest authors in the world at that time.

So, even though I hate flying and I am a nervous tourist, I am so glad I took that trip. Lou has very much inspired me to just get out and do shit.

Doing big overseas trips is amazing, however, deep down I think what Europe and America have taught me is that I'm super Australian. I love the warmth and the water and it's where I am at my happiest. If I had the option of a week in Noosa or a trip to the Maldives, I would have to say I think I'd take Noosa. I think. Unless Lou was paying.

Part Three

ADULTING

9

FLYING THE COOP

There comes a time in every young man's life where he must step out from the shadows of his parents and into the light— and move the fuck out of home. By the time this day came around for me, it is fair to say I had well and truly outstayed my welcome. Mum and Dad only have themselves to blame, though—they made our home too comfortable and our fridge way too well-stocked for me to ever want to leave, even if I was constantly having to invent creative reasons for leaving the house late in the evening for Grindr hook-ups. There are only so many times you can return a library book at ten pm.

And when I finally did leave, it was not even because I had decided I was ready—it was for a job. It all started when, after having worked in retail for five years and spending three summers as a camp counsellor in America, I decided at the ripe old age of twenty-three that it was time for me to get my shit together.

As well as slogging it out in retail, I'd been working in community radio for four years and was both hosting a breakfast show on Mondays, Wednesdays and Fridays on 2RRR in Gladesville in Sydney's Lower North Shore and volunteering as a coordinator at FBi 94.5 radio in inner-city Redfern. So while working in retail was slowly destroying my soul, my real satisfaction and drive was all about radio. I knew it was where I wanted my future to be.

I decided I would apply to study radio at the Australian Film, Television and Radio School (aka AFTRS), an elite college for arty-farty types in Sydney. The AFTRS radio course took just over a dozen students a year and it was an intense, competitive and highly sought-after course whose graduates pretty much walked into positions at regional radio stations across Australia. I had applied straight out of school in 2004 and was turned away due to a lack of industry experience. It was now 2009 and I had a heap of knowledge up my sleeve. If I didn't get in this time around, there was no hope.

If I had to say one thing to people wanting to get into the entertainment world in whatever field, it would probably be to go and find somewhere to volunteer. Those years volunteering on community radio were honestly the best years of my life. It was unbelievably fun and rewarding, I learned HEAPS and I met the most amazing people—people who to this day have continued to support me in my career and have my back. A special shout-out here to Meagan, FBi's program director when I volunteered there, who basically got me into the AFTRS radio course. It's not what you know but who you know, as they say!

Meagan might have put in a good word for me, but once the course started I was on my own. This was an intense course— six days a week, nine to five. Who would have thought you needed to do so much work to talk into a stick!

It was so much fun and the group of us were all so different and had loud personalities, as you can imagine. Our first major assignment was to build and run a radio station at the Sydney Royal Easter Show. It was called Show Radio and we had to do pretty much all the work in getting it on air. Recording sound effects ('sweepers' as they are known in the biz), building ads and promos and hosting shows and doing interviews. It was so full-on. It was live for two weeks.

We had to find twelve hours of content per day for the show. We milked every little thing we could to do so. How to eat a dagwood dog without gagging! The best way to push in a cow's prolapsed uterus! Guess the showbag! And, my personal favourite, what animal dung is this? You name it, we did it. When those two weeks were up we all wanted to take a six-month holiday, but we were straight back into the thick of it with more classes.

LEAVE US ALONE! Why are we learning about sales? We all have aspirations of forward announcing the new Taylor

Swift song, not of knowing how much ads cost and why sales are important. NO ONE IS HERE TO LEARN ABOUT SALES!

This might sound controversial, but I'm pretty sure I was dux of the class. Pippa and Reegan were the two 'give no fucks' cool kids and I was the teacher's pet. I made the teachers gifts and quite literally brought them apples every day. I then tried to appear like I was one of the cool kids and hung out with Reegan and Pippa. Reegan was the first guy who I openly talked about gay stuff with.

He was gay, but you couldn't tell. So when I found out, I almost died. I'm pretty sure he had the hots for me. I mean, who wouldn't have? (See any of the pics in this book, especially the one of me with bleached blonde hair, for proof.)

Reegan did something that no one had ever done for me before. He got angry on my behalf. Basically, he stood up and defended me. I didn't realise why at the time, but as an adult now looking back, I can see that it was the right thing to do. I should have said something myself, but I didn't. Let me explain.

We had a voice coach come in to listen to each of us and tell us what she thought about our sound. She was super lovely, helped us identify and address any bad voice habits or mannerisms and improved our diction. This was all done in front of the rest of the class. When I got up and spoke, her advice was that I needed to lower my voice. I'm naturally high-pitched and very camp. So she got me to do some exercises to change how I sounded. Sadly, this is pretty commonplace in radio. If you're a man, you need a deep voice. You need to hide the camp and be a manly man.

I was going through these exercises in front of everyone, thinking nothing of it. I was so keen to get into radio, I would have done anything, frankly. I was willing to change how I sounded. I had done some exercises and was finishing up when I was advised to continue working on these exercises outside of class in order to perfect that lower register in my voice.

Cue Reegan. He stood up and proclaimed that this was bullshit. He told the class and the teachers that this was disgusting, that he was infuriated that I should be made to conform and that he wanted no part in this whole shitshow. Being a person who just wants everyone to get along and not realising the deeper meaning behind his outburst, I tried to manage the situation by telling him that I was fine with it. This is one of my regrets in life and I think my response came from a lack of understanding. I wish I had the confidence back then to say NO! You get what you get. I'm high-pitched and sound like my mother—bad luck! I'm not changing.

Reegan was absolutely right. While this moment may not have had a huge impact on him, it has absolutely stuck with me. For years, that day played in my head. It gave me the courage to question people if I felt something was off and also gave me the confidence to just be myself.

Reegan, I know you're reading this as you no doubt have messaged me asking for a free copy. I want to say thank you!

It was honestly a really life-changing moment. As a token of my gratitude, you can have this book for free. Please send $8.95 postage.

Graduating from the class was an amazing feeling. My high school graduation experience had been a bit touch-and-go and I didn't do so good, but when I got my radio diploma, I was very proud—as were my parents. I'm pretty sure they were mostly just shocked that I was even able to get a diploma.

After graduating AFTRS, I applied for and, much to my surprise, landed a job out at Young in central New South Wales, a good four-hour drive from Sydney.

Not only was I leaving home (at last), I was going rural! I was so excited to start work! I'd been given the breakfast timeslot of six am to nine am. I bragged to every person I knew (and some I didn't know), packed up all my gear and hit the road. It was all so full of promise. Surely in a small town like Young, being on the radio would make you pretty much a local celebrity. I wondered how much free stuff I would get. The world was my oyster! Or so I thought.

Now, in hindsight, allow me to summarise for you the experience of a gay city boy going rural: SCARY AS HELL.

I moved into a tiny one-bedroom townhouse that I had been excited about making the first ever home of my very own, but I had never felt more isolated in my life. I like my own space, but this was too much of my own space. There was no one. The work was okay and the people were nice, but it wasn't enough. The difference between being alone in a city and being alone in the country was real: in the city, when you leave the house, it is total chaos. There are events and functions happening, people every-fucking-where and the city is alive with activity. While I usually avoided all of this activity, preferring to stay in the safety of my couch, at least I knew it was there and always would be if I needed it. But in Young, there was literally nothing. It is a beautiful country town and the landscape is stunning, however, for me, going from such craziness, as well as living with a close-knit family and having a busy studying schedule, to complete isolation just wasn't healthy.

I lasted three weeks and had a breakdown. It all came to a head when I was doing an outside broadcast show from a market. I was outside, mingling with people and talking about tractors and stuff I had no idea about. One older guy walked straight up to me and asked me a few questions about being 'a gay'. I felt so uncomfortable and just knew I needed to get out. He was respectful, but in a weird condescending way. Keep in mind this was my first taste of the real world. It was such a dramatic shift. Small country towns are all about community and everyone knows everyone. I was welcomed, but due to my own insecurities I just felt very out of place. I couldn't handle it.

For the first three weeks, not having a clue how to cope, I had made heaps of phone calls to friends and lecturers asking their advice regarding what I should do. Should I leave? They all said the same thing: 'Just stick it out—this is how radio works.' But I just couldn't do it. I felt depression and loneliness creep in and I stopped eating. Talk about a red flag. All I wanted was for someone to tell me it was okay to throw in the towel. I just needed that reassurance. But I wasn't getting it from anyone.

Then, as a last resort, I called Mum and Dad. For some reason, I thought they would be the hardest to convince. I had avoided having this conversation with them because three weeks isn't long and I was positive they would say, 'Just see how you go for another month.' But I called them and I'm pretty sure they could tell from the sound of my voice that I wasn't in the best of places. 'We are coming to get you,' they said. And just like that, my radio dream was shattered and I was back living at home and working in retail.

When I got home, I was in shock. I'd been so sure that this was it for me—moving to Young for a radio job was my moment and I was going to shine. But despite all the hard work and the years of community radio, I'd failed. Going back to work in a homewares shop was almost a relief. The pressure was off, I was at home and back to a routine I was familiar with. I felt disappointed that all that work and my fantasy radio career were now lost to the ages, but I knew I'd find something else. Maybe I would go back and work in America again.

It turned out not to be the end of my story, thank god. After a few months back in retail, I got a call from a lecturer at AFTRS saying he had put me forward for a job in Newcastle as a panel operator for the radio station NXFM. It wasn't an on-air job, but it was still a good opportunity.

The job was as basic as you can get. I literally just had to watch a computer screen to make sure the radio station didn't go off-air. Newcastle is a lot closer to Sydney than Young, but the commute would be seventy-five minutes each way. It was a big drive, but this was a big opportunity. I was pretty sure I could handle it. I told Mum and Dad and they were thrilled. The plan was to still live in Sydney and just drive up for each shift. I had about three shifts a week, starting at four pm and finishing at ten pm.

I loved every second of every minute of that job. Newcastle is a great environment to be in, being a beachside town, and the team I worked with was incredible.

Day one, I was shown how to panel by a young guy from Brisbane who had been working at NXFM for about a year. I was *very* distracted by his good looks. He was a water polo player, so he was tall and toned. He was also young, only about nineteen. Jack was really the first proper straight male friend I ever had. We worked closely together for the next couple of years. I owe him a lot, as without him I wouldn't have found my feet and would still be wandering the halls of NXFM looking for the bathroom.

We had a lot of fun. One thing to know about Jack is that he rather liked getting *almost* naked a lot. No complaints from me! One time, he wanted to recreate a music video in which a near-naked hot chick washes a car. Obviously, I was all for helping Jack do this. He put on some tiny white speedos and proceeded to wash the NXFM car. I literally filmed what could rightly be considered softcore porn with Jack as the star—all while getting paid! This job was awesome.

Did I save the footage? Yes. Do I still have the footage? You bet your fucking ass I do.

Another hilarious Jack moment was when he hid under the desk in the radio studio with the intention of trying to scare me. Another colleague and I walked into the studio, me not knowing Jack was under the desk, and my colleague asked me if I thought Jack was hot. What a set-up! Here is what I said: 'Yes, he is hot. Great body. Shame about his dick of a personality though.'

Then I got the shock of my life when a dude jumped up from under the desk and scared me. First, I just screamed from shock, and then I realised it was Jack and screamed even louder. Had he heard what I'd just said? If so, he didn't seem to care! He wasn't exactly lacking in confidence and I think he already knew that I thought he was hot. I'm not particularly good at hiding it. The giveaway was probably that whenever he would tell a joke, I'd laugh extra loud and gently touch his hand.

Jack and I never did make it to third base, or even first base. He ended up marrying the most stunning woman I have ever seen. She is so lovely. I'm not jealous. Stop looking at me!

The Newcastle years were some of the best years of my life. I think the bigger city, the beach and being so close to home was what made it different to my Young experience. Also, there are a lot of gays in Newcastle. I had a lot of sex. Always a bonus.

I went from a little inexperienced panel op (button pusher) to working on the breakfast show playing the role of a character called 'The Fairy'. Again, not totally PC but I loved it—I got to dress up in a fairy outfit and prance around Newcastle giving away big prizes and doing crazy stunts for the Steve & Kim breakfast show. It rated really well and I became a little bit of a local celebrity. This was my first taste of fame and it made me hungry for more.

Three years into my stint in Newcastle, Jack got a job in Adelaide at SAFM. He ended up convincing the bosses there to hire me as his assistant and I made the decision to take the job and move from the stunning area of Lake Macquarie to the posh Adelaide suburb of Unley. The next step in my radio career had begun but sadly it wasn't to go as planned.

10

SPREADING MY WINGS

So, there I was, twenty-five years old and about to take the biggest leap of faith so far in my career. The bad experience I had in Young was long behind me, and over the three years at Newcastle's NXFM I had not only advanced my skills—learning to host a show and get my on-air experience up, as well as how to schedule music for a radio station—but I had also really settled into my own skin. Part of this had to do with work—I fit in with the team and achieved a lot there—but a big part of it was also down to the fact that I'd had to stand on my own two feet and make it work in Newcastle, and I had done it.

When Jack got me the job in Adelaide, I knew instantly that I wanted to accept it. For all that I had done in Newcastle, I had begun to feel like I was standing still, and my weeks (and hook-ups, let's be honest) had started to feel like groundhog day. I knew it was time for a change, and I really liked the idea of going interstate. Adelaide seemed like it was the right next step: not too big, but not too small—and plenty of new faces on Grindr. Also, at that time, I had no idea the bogong moth even existed. Would I have gone to Adelaide if I had known of its giant moth infestation? FUCK NO!

Adelaide ended up being an eye-opening experience in many ways. I started out as assistant music director to Jack, which basically involved me helping him schedule music and meet with big record companies and artists, but mostly doing a lot of admin work. I wanted so badly to be on air but was happy to start with being the assistant music director alongside Jack. It was a fun team and a great environment. It was the first big metro commercial radio station I had worked at— something that had been a dream of mine for years—and that meant it worked a bit differently to what I had become used to and I learned heaps.

By differently, I mean you weren't as easily forgiven if you made a mistake. In Newcastle, I was constantly taking the station off air. Basically nothing would be playing for a while because I was down in the kitchen eating food and had forgotten to turn a few switches and so when a song finished, it didn't go to the next song and nothing would play. I would then bolt up the hall and burst into the studio and frantically push all the buttons to make something play. This is very frowned upon usually, but in Newy I got away with doing this almost daily.

In Adelaide, however, if the station went off air, an alert went to almost every member of the management team and there were calls and meetings and you were issued a warning. I needed to pay close attention to everything. I still took the station off air a few times, but I used my charm to not get fired.

However, after about three good months there, Jack got promoted to the company's Melbourne station, FoxFM, and left Adelaide. Everything changed. I realised I was not cut out to step into the role of music director and things for me started to crumble. I was given the responsibility of scheduling the music for SAFM, but instead of replacing Jack as the official music director, I was to perform all the same tasks but for less money and under the guidance of three people. This 'guidance' in fact ended up being absolute hell. It was less guide-like and more like a three-way tug of war, with me flapping about somewhere in the middle.

Let me break down how music is scheduled for a radio station. It's a science—a totally made-up, subjective and often bullshit science. There are so many rules on each song and so many rules on how they should be sequenced. Are you confused? I don't blame you. But to cut a long story short: one song can't necessarily just be played after any old other song—the program must follow a set of weird and sometimes completely random scheduling rules, and there are certain songs that have to be programmed at certain times, targets to hit and boxes to check off. And all of this has to be coded and timed and listed and marked off and offered up to the crazy programming gods, preferably while also drawing blood and reciting pi to eighteen decimal places with a broom up your ass. AND YOU CANNOT BREAK THESE RULES OR THE WORLD WILL COLLAPSE.

Imagine little Christian, sitting at a computer making playlists all fucking day and then having three people look at them and all three people saying they are wrong and offering their own hot take on how to fix them. I'd show one person and they would make me move and change songs, then the next person would take a look, completely contradict the first person, then finally, review number three would happen and I'd be told to basically change it back to what I had originally. I was in a living hell. This would happen day after day. How was I supposed to learn when I had people contradicting each other? One day, I had had enough. It was crushing my soul and depressing me. It ended with me quitting and in tears again, my radio dream in tatters.

My boss at the time, Donna, was a bit of a lifesaver for me and when I told her I couldn't continue on as 'makeshift' music director, she pulled some strings to make me a producer of a new breakfast show SAFM was going to be announcing in the coming weeks. Donna knew me well and I am one hundred per cent sure that deep down she was just doing me a favour, as I am the most useless and untrainable human on the planet. I am sure she knew this was going to be a lot of work for her. She was about to have a useless junior producer working on a brand-new show.

After eighteen months on that show, I was still a shit producer. My job was being the phone bitch for Michael, Hayley and Burgo, the on-air hosts. This involved putting calls through to the studio and, boy, was I the worst candidate for the job. You have to be quick and on the ball to be a phone bitch. I was neither of those things. I was a little gay boy who wanted to be the on-air talent but who had been relegated to the phones—that is, I was a recipe for disaster. I couldn't spell to save my life and often when I put a call through to the studio, they'd have no idea what I had written on the note. This made for horrible radio and I was blamed and rightly so. My heart wasn't in it. I hated the job and it was becoming increasingly obvious to not just me but everyone else as well.

I was on the verge of quitting again, but I knew this time there would be no one to save me and no going back, so I pushed through. It's really fucking hard to wake up at four forty-five am to go to a job you hate. The only saving grace was that I just had to get to nine am and the show would finish. It was like that feeling when church finishes: you have the longest time before more church.

Then the company who owned the station I worked for, SCA, made a bunch of redundancies in the online/digital department—a part of the business I knew next to nothing about. Included in the redundancies was a guy called Tyson, the local office eye candy—a tall, fit and attractive Swedish blond. He'd been in charge of the website and getting stuff up on Facebook.

I ended up picking up the slack left by Tyson's departure. This was the moment I first picked up a small handy-cam and began to film Michael, Hayley and Burgo. I would film the pranks we would play and edit up little videos to post online. This was fun. I finally had a creative outlet. I enjoyed the filming and editing process a lot. However, I wasn't doing this very often and I was also still the phone bitch.

This was the moment I had unknowingly begun my career as a digital video producer. This was the moment that I truly discovered what I wanted to do for a job. I didn't yet realise it, but I had found my calling.

Donna ended up leaving and going to run 2Day FM and we got a new boss, Jase. He was only a few years older than me and the most immature boss I have ever had. In a good way. He would often scream at me in an aggressive tone to 'get into my office right now . . . and shut the door'. Then we would go through an archive of radio bloopers he had saved over the years and end up crying with laughter. My desk was outside his office and sometimes I would hear a loud bang just above my head, which was him throwing objects at me in order to scare me. He had a ninety per cent success rate— I would always scream in the most camp way and then throw things back at him.

Jase walked into SAFM at a critical time for me. I was at the end of it all, ready to walk. I was emotionally and mentally drained from my five am starts and from working a job I wasn't right for. I was in tears in his office a few times, and on the 600th time I told him I couldn't do it anymore and that I wanted out.

I got out. I went from full-time to casual. It was the best and most wise and healthy career decision I have ever made. Thankfully for me, money was not going to be a problem, as I had some savings from not having spent much over the past few years when my life was basically all work.

I had made enough of an impact at SAFM that I was able to get lots of casual shifts on the street team and panelling late-night shows. I was also still filming and editing videos for the breakfast show. This was what I loved doing. I wanted to make a career of it, but nothing really existed in that area yet. You have to remember this was still the early days of businesses even using Facebook.

Jase was very supportive over this time and, partly to repay his faith in me, I really put my head down and worked hard in my various roles. Then it happened. My breakthrough moment. It was a Saturday and I had gone in to work to pick up some stuff from my desk. I was online and noticed a story break about a famous Aussie athlete being rushed to hospital. I noticed no other news sites had picked up the story, so I wrote it up and published it on our website. The story ended up getting 12,000 hits (a huge number for us at the time), which was noticed by our head of digital. She got in touch with me and we got talking about my role at SAFM and what I wanted to do in my career.

I ended up getting in front of the massive big digital boss for SCA and I told him what I wanted to do. Next minute, I was flown to Melbourne to interview for a huge position on a national drive show. A NATIONAL FUCKING DRIVE SHOW. The pinnacle of success is working on a national drive show. I had no chance of getting the job, but an interview was amazing. It's like being nominated for an Oscar: you know you won't win but just a nomination is totally worth it.

It turns out there were no other candidates and by default I got the job. FUCK, I LOVE DEFAULT!!!

The Oscar for Best Use of Default goes to . . . [envelope opens] . . . Oh, I'm the only nominee!

11

THE BIG TIME

It was April 2014 and the move to Melbourne was a big one. I had landed the role of National Digital Video Producer for the drive show, which at the time was hosted by Dan and Maz. This was the big time. It didn't get any bigger than this. I was underprepared and had no idea what I was walking into, however I quickly realised this was going to be the most amazing gig of my life and it really was.

My first week I was thrown into it. First up, I was to film an interview with Ed Sheeran in a limo. OH, IS THAT ALL? This was where I met another key player in my career. Blake was a bit of a heavyweight in the digital video world and the first person I had ever met who was making a career out of it. We had first met in Adelaide a few months prior when he was flown over to talk about the future direction of digital. He ended up being my lifeline when I was working on the Dan & Maz Show. Blake taught me everything I needed to know to get through my first three months. He taught me to edit, shoot and the all-important art of lighting.

On top of landing well and truly on my feet with my dream gig and an incredible mentor, Melbourne also really seemed to suit me. I got a nice apartment in a posh inner-city suburb and set myself up pretty well, surrounded by my favourite things: four walls and a door to block out the outside world.

The job was high pressure, but really exciting. Dan and Maz were loud and polar opposite. Dan was nerdy—think *Dungeons & Dragons*–level nerdiness—and Maz was cool, she had worked at MTV and just oozed that trendy vibe. She was delightful too, a real sweetheart. They were great fun to be around.

I have a loud and annoying laugh, so it was no surprise I bonded with Carly, the senior producer of the show. She gave me a run for my money. The two of us together rivalled the sound of a jackhammer. We would often just laugh at how loud we were. I would like to say that I, however, was the one voted as having the best laugh in the office!

I would tell you what an average day working there involved, but really there was no such thing as an average day. It was adrenaline-pumping and hectic and I barely had time to catch my breath, let alone take in everything that was going on around me and how much I was learning.

I met heaps of celebrities and some of them were amazing. Two big celeb names stand out to me for how damn nice they were.

First, Slash from Guns N' Roses. In walked this tall, big-haired, insanely famous musician. He said hello to everyone in the studio, shook all their hands and introduced himself. I was tucked away behind a camera in the corner of the radio studio, getting the shot set up. He didn't see me and sadly I didn't get a handshake. Then, just before the interview started, he noticed me there and then got up, came over, apologised and said hi to me! WHO DOES THAT? That really stuck with me.

I like to think that if I ever get that famous, I will remember Slash and embody the same kind of gracious humility that he showed on that day. WHO AM I FUCKING KIDDING! I totally will *not* be like that at all. I'll be more like the celebrity* who refused to acknowledge me and then demanded I get them a glass of chilled water. They had an entourage of seven people and yet I was the one who was barked at to fetch the water, and *then*, when I handed it to them, they refused to take it, refused to say thank you and were just a real dick. Turns out I really hold on to things, hey! Seriously though, how hard is it to just say hello and thank you?

*My lawyers made me remove their name.

The other surprisingly nice celeb who I met was the big kahuna herself: Kim Kardashian. The day we interviewed Kim, I was (again) hiding in my corner of the studio behind the camera waiting for KK's arrival. In walked about five people—and one of them was Kim. She was tiny and gorgeous and very softly spoken. She sat down and I noticed her assistant quietly indicate to Kim where the cameras were. Kim looked over in my direction, smiled and then perfectly positioned her body and hair to give me THE MOST amazing shot of her. Usually I had to move the camera multiple times, give the celeb some direction about how to sit and where to look and adjust everything around for a while to set up a nice shot, but being the pro that she is, that day Kim did my job for me. She was so down-to-earth and very polite.

Another huge perk of the job was that we often had musicians and artists come in to perform their hit songs. These were always pre-recorded just outside our radio studio in what we called the airlock—an open space where the producers sat when the show was on air. It was a pretty small room, so when artists performed in there everyone would leave the airlock to give them space and also to eliminate annoying background noise during the performance. I, however, would stay in the airlock armed with my camera to film the performance for us to post online later. It was a completely surreal experience, as I was literally the only one there. It always felt to me like they were performing their song just for me. In many cases, I believe they felt the same way. We had artists like George Ezra, G.R.L, Little Mix and Fifth Harmony all perform—just for me!

IT WAS SO AMAZING.

The Dan & Maz Show was a show like no other. It was different, unique and so weird, I loved it. Sadly, it was a good time and not a long time, as after only working on the show for seven months, Hamish and Andy wanted back in the game, so Dan and Maz were moved from their national four to six pm slot to the breakfast shift in Sydney.

I naturally thought I would move with the show to Sydney, so I was devastated to find out they would not be taking me with them. I understood the reasoning: their new show was high stakes for them both and it *had* to work. This was not a station or a timeslot that they could afford to take a gamble on 'the new kid' with—they needed someone more experienced, someone with actual skills.

If you are familiar with the 2Day FM breakfast show curse, you will know that I dodged a bullet. This was a timeslot vacated by my idols, Kyle and Jackie O. To this day, it has never recovered from their departure in its ratings and it is known for being brutal. Something I didn't know at the time. In an odd twist of fate, I would actually accept a job on the 2Day FM breakfast show a few years later (in 2017) and in true cursed fashion, it was brutal and not the greatest experience.

But in 2014, I stayed in Melbourne and jumped around working on a few different shows until I landed a role as the digital producer on an experimental show called *YouTube Hits* with Michael Beveridge and Marty Smiley. It was a nightly two-hour pre-recorded show that was all about what was happening on YouTube. And it wasn't just a radio show—it was also an actual YouTube show. I filmed segments and uploaded them to our YouTube channel. The show was the brainchild of my old mentor, Blake. His idea was to integrate radio with YouTube in a cool and unique way. It was a really successful show and we got huge numbers on YouTube. It was for the most part a really fun experience. I worked the hardest I had ever worked and at times felt like I was a mindless zombie consistently filming and editing for up to fourteen hours a day.

After spending 2015 working on *YouTube Hits*, I decided to start my own channels on YouTube, Facebook and Instagram. Everything I had learned over the past year was extremely beneficial. How to edit videos in a certain way, what content people liked watching and how to actually publish properly online—all of this knowledge gave me the confidence to start up my own channels and feel like I vaguely knew what I was doing. I also started my own podcast, *Complete Drivel*, which was basically just me talking unscripted shit about whatever the hell I wanted to. It was fun to do and I enjoyed learning the technical skills of podcasting too. I didn't have many listeners to start with, but I was doing it for the experience, to be creative and to have fun, so I didn't care.

I continued to work on *YouTube Hits* until it wrapped up suddenly in 2016. Sadly, the show just hadn't been popular enough with management and they pulled the plug. They just didn't understand the format, really. It was a perfect example of the whole mainstream media versus social media tension. Which was sad because if they'd stuck with it, I reckon it could have been huge. It was an amazing show, super experimental and I believe ahead of its time.

At the end of 2016, miraculously still employed by SCA, I got a call from another radio station. It came on Christmas Eve. This was the call that I had dreamed of getting for so many years. It was to see if I would like to work on the Kyle and Jackie O Show. My entire radio dream was based around Kyle. I grew up listening to Kyle and Jackie O and I always wanted to work on their show. Say what you like about him, he knows how to entertain! My mum hates him, but often says I'm like a smaller, gayer version of him.

I was told what the job would be and the pay (which was insanely good) and was given a week to make a decision. I was on holidays back home in Sydney with the family when this all happened. I had never felt so confident and happy. This was such a turning point in my life: finally I got to call the shots about where I would go and what I wanted to do. I had people I idolised wanting me to work on their shows!

I called my boss at SCA, Chris, the head of digital. Chris was one of those bosses who actually cared about you. He had looked out for me on countless occasions and had my back when I needed it. I really loved working with him and knew deep down I couldn't just walk out after everything he had done for me. However, the offer from KIIS to work with Kyle and Jackie O was too big to ignore. And really good money!

Here is how my decision looked: option one was to stay in Melbourne and work on the new 2Day FM breakfast show with Em and Harley as their digital producer. Option two was to move back to Sydney and work at KIIS as its digital video lead with a heavy focus on the Kyle and Jackie O Show.

I adored living in Melbourne—it was a vibrant, easy, super liveable city. I had an insanely awesome apartment and the cost of rent was (compared to Sydney) super cheap. But Sydney was home and my family was there. I had always wanted to be independent in Sydney, have an apartment in Balmain and be super posh. I would be able to afford to do that with this new job.

And there was one other thing: even though this was literally a dream come true, the timing was completely off. If they'd made the call to me three years earlier, I would have absolutely said yes in an instant. But now I had other things to consider as well and the biggest thing tugging at the corners of my mind was that I had been doing my own Facebook and YouTube channels for over a year and a half, and things had been going beyond my expectations.

In fact, part of the reason I even got the call from KIIS was because of the success of my Facebook page. But if I accepted this job in Sydney, it would be so full-on that I most likely just wouldn't have the time or energy to keep up with my own content.

So I spoke to Chris about my options and he was honest about what it would mean if I moved. I was absolutely spoiled at SCA—we had the best digital team in the country and the support for its growth in the business was huge. A move to

KIIS just couldn't be as golden as it was at SCA, he was right. I was so happy at SCA and in Melbourne and it had taken me twelve years of working in community and commercial radio around Australia to get to this golden point. I decided to stay.

I was excited to work on a new show at 2Day FM too—everything seemed to be pointing towards it being an awesome year. I said no to KIIS and I stayed in Melbourne with SCA. I have never regretted that decision.

And even though 2017 ended up being one of my toughest years, it also had enormous highs. My Facebook page had a huge surge in numbers and the podcast I started the year before made it to the top ten on iTunes.

But working on the 2Day FM breakfast show was a hard-core experience. I thought I knew what hard work was, but this was something else. There's just no way to explain how gruelling and isolating it was.

Being a video producer is fun work and it sounds easy. Just film some stuff then pop it up online. This couldn't be further from the truth. But I still loved the job—we had the most engaged Facebook and Instagram accounts in the network.

Some experiences are best left in the past and that's where I want to leave this one. The classic 2Day FM breakfast show curse strikes again.

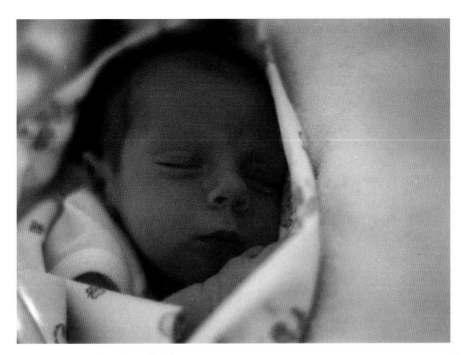

An eight-day-old alien child.

Obviously I was a great baby—my parents look so well rested. I also love Dad's shirt and Mum's hair.

Leslie and George's (AKA Nan and Pa) pool in Lindfield, NSW. So many fights with my brothers took place in this pool.

The annual Christmas photo that took about 60 goes to get one good one.

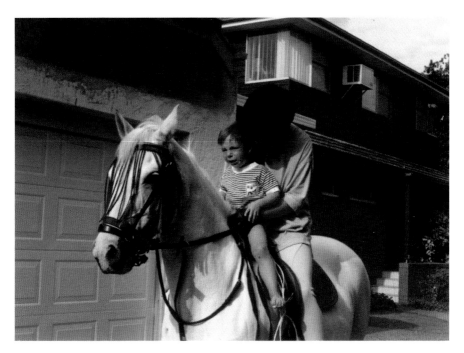

Having a great time on our neighbour's scary horse . . .

Alan and Joan (Pa and Nanna Joan), with Aunty Gen and my cousin Jess. Mum is up the back and the three little shits and I are in the front row.

My favourite photo of my brothers.

Year Twelve, me and Chantelle. We used to wag school. We look so rebellious!

My best friend Ashleigh, seen here tolerating me.

The famous red Nissan Pulsar and the boys: Pa, Dad and my brothers.

Hosting the breakfast show on community station 2RRR in Gladesville, NSW.

A nineteen-year-old me with bleached blond hair, in California as a camp counsellor.

My 21st birthday with my best friends Trudy (in red) and Jen (in the glasses), holding little four-year-old Mia with my friend Sandra up the back.

My brothers and two of their soon-to-be wives, Jenny and Holly, doing the Harbour Bridge Climb for my birthday.

The radio dream team: working on the Carrie & Tommy show.

Working on the Dan & Maz drive show and meeting my idol, Jenna Marbles.

Bringing my family up on stage after finishing the last show on my first big national comedy tour.

Best mates in New York, me and Emmylou.

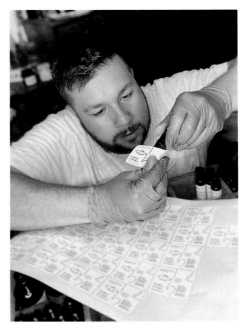

Labelling my bestselling fragrance, Farqovski.

12

VIDEO KILLED THE RADIO DREAM

For as long as I can remember, I have always wanted to be famous. What an arrogant, soulless, superficial dream! But it's absolutely what I wanted. From an early age, I loved attention. Loved performing, showing off and forcing people to watch my dumb plays. I was absolutely adored by my parents—maybe it was all this love and admiration I felt as a kid that led to me wanting to be famous. I feel a real sense of shallowness admitting to it but wanting to be famous was my main dream growing up. Not famous for anything in particular, just famous. Not talented, just goddamn famous.

Mum even has a video of me as a kid in which she asks me what I want to be when I grow up and I say straight to camera: 'I want to be famous.' I just think I always wanted to entertain and I understood that to be the job of famous people.

I vividly remember my first taste of the spotlight—it was a total disaster. I was in Year Three, I believe, about seven years old and my primary school was performing in a big variety show, to be held at the local high school on this massive stage. It was just a showcase of all the different year groups and my class's number must have been something Roman as I was dressed as a gladiator, wearing sandals with shoelaces up my calves and some sort of red, brown and gold number.

The stage was tiered, so the front row of kids would be on the actual stage and the second row were up on a step. To get up into the second row, you had to step up on a carpeted box with metal-trimmed edges. I was in the middle in the second row and as I stepped up to my spot, I slipped and hit my shin on the metal trim of the box. I was so embarrassed that I didn't realise I had gashed my shin open and blood was pouring out. I just stood there and tried not to cry from the shame I had brought to myself, to my class and to my whole school and my family. I completely forgot all the words to the song we were singing and spent the performance just moving my mouth, vaguely miming and haemorrhaging from the leg. I just couldn't wait for the nightmare to be over.

We were on stage singing for about four minutes in total, enough time for my sandal to fill with blood and for the blood to start overflowing onto the carpet. I wasn't faint from nerves, I was faint from the huge blood loss I was unaware of. We finished and as I walked off stage, I could feel a squelching in my shoe. I looked down to see a puddle of my blood pooled on the stage that I was trailing after me with every footstep.

I remember seeing skin hanging and then crying in the wings and blacking out. I have no further memory of that horrific night. I believe that the show was put on hold for a few minutes and that everything was mopped up, so the Year Fours didn't have to splash around in my blood for their performance. Ironically, they were doing *Singin' in the Rain*, and a touch of real blood would have made for a very post-modern performance.

After that, in terms of my on-stage experience, the only way was up. If the performance didn't end with a stage soaked in my blood and me blacking out, then it was a win!

But this love of performing was gradually snuffed out of me as I grew up—probably mostly due to my pretty shitty high school experience. I always knew that I loved making people laugh, but there was a lot I needed to come to terms with about myself before I could step out on stage and perform. I needed to work out who I was before I could showcase it to the world.

For a while, I found that spark again when I was volunteering on air on community radio—a spark that ultimately led me to taking the plunge to study at AFTRS. But shortly after that my confidence got another huge knock in Young, and since then I had relegated myself to behind-the-scenes and producing roles. I was happy because I was still working in radio *with* famous people who were amazing talents, but deep down

I knew that I wanted to be more than behind the scenes—
I wanted to *be* the scene!

I had wanted to start creating my own content online
for a while before I actually did, but procrastination had got
the better of me. When I was working on *YouTube Hits*, we
would often interview huge YouTubers who had millions of
subscribers and they would all say the same thing: 'Just start!
You won't start out on a million followers, no one does. But
you have to actually start.'

In the end, I bit the bullet and took their advice. My early
videos are fucking terrible. It was through trial and error that
I discovered what worked and what I liked making—mostly
short, relatable and funny sketches, which I would upload onto
Facebook. I loved making them even though the only person
who was watching and laughing at them was me. I was my
own biggest fan. Such a narcissist! To this day, I will happily
watch my own content and laugh. It's just that these days,
other people might also watch and laugh. This was not the
case back then—it was just me, myself and I! I told nobody
about my page for a few weeks, as I was scared people would
find out just how unfunny I was. That old self-doubt from
high school that had taken me almost a decade to shrug off
threatened to rear its ugly head at every turn, and often did.

It didn't help that I wasn't actually getting a heap of cut
through and, being the super impatient person I am, I had
expected my content to reach the masses overnight. So,
I did what all major attention-seekers have done since time

immemorial: I hatched a plan to solve this problem. My employer at the time, SCA, had a Facebook page for every station in the network and these pages had huge numbers of followers, between 400,000 and 600,000 per page. I had access to all of these pages as I was producing and posting video content all the time for the shows I worked on. We often shared videos to these Facebook pages from other creators— so I thought to myself: 'I'm a creator, why can't we share my videos?'

I was smart enough to keep this idea to myself and I just went in and began to share my own videos on these pages. I told no one what I was doing and I would share them late at night when I thought no one from work would notice. Crazily enough, it started to work. My videos did really well and my own page began to build a pretty good following of its own. It turned out that quite a few people at the station did know what I was doing, but they looked the other way and let me get away with it. There did come a time where I was kindly asked to stop (awkward!) and I agreed. I was fine with it, as by that stage I had about 20,000 followers and a nice little audience to communicate with.

Then something magical happened. I found Trish.

For those who don't know who Trish is, she is an alter-ego character I have played in many of my videos and she is pretty much the reason for my success.

Discovering Trish wasn't a big moment. She made her first appearance in a little sketch and I thought nothing of it. Then I made another video with her and she just started to grow into this character. Trish doesn't really have a back-story and she isn't someone with a consistent timeline. She is basically whatever I need her to be at the time: a mum, a flight attendant or a bogan. But Trish really took on a life of her own when I started to make the angry mum content. She became my go-to character to play a mum of two annoying kids. I made little videos about what it was like getting kids ready for school, driving with kids, taking the kids shopping— just the mundane day-to-day stuff mums have to deal with, really. They are based largely on my own childhood and the things Dad would yell at us growing up. I thought my parents were the only parents who screamed at their kids one hundred per cent of the time. NOPE! This was all parents—this is what parenting is actually like. With Trish, I had unwittingly tapped into something universal. People just loved her.

I was still sitting on about 20,000 followers and at this point had received no money from what I was doing—it was simply an outlet for me to create stuff. I hadn't even thought about this getting any bigger and I certainly hadn't thought I could make any money from it.

The moment everything changed was a Trish video I made about being a nurse. I got a message from a guy in New Zealand who listed a bunch of things that happen in his daily life as a nurse and it was so funny. The sketch pretty much wrote itself. When I filmed this video, I didn't expect it to do so well.

It is to date my most watched video and the video that got my Facebook page in front of so many people. After the nurse video, things took off really quickly and my followers grew to 200,000 in three months. It was so motivating to see the number grow so quickly. It can also pull you in a deep rabbit hole of obsession, though, and I found myself constantly looking at my analytics, always checking to see how many people had viewed which videos and basing my sense of success on my view count. Not the best place to be.

I loved that my Trish videos brought some sort of sanity to parents. I often have people stop me in the street to tell me they have teenagers and my videos are an account of their everyday life. It made them feel normal; their stressful lives were given validation by these videos. The comments section is always fun to read after I post something. It's like a competition for who has the worst kid.

Trish opened so many doors for me. She put me in front of so many eyes. Two sets of important eyes that Trish put me in front of belonged to Luke Girgis, who runs The Brag Media, and one of his employees, Sarah. Before I had really blown up on Facebook, I'd received a call from them inquiring if I had any management and if getting a manager was something that I had considered. Luke and Sarah are two of the most supportive people I have ever come across and they saw a huge benefit in me partnering up with them. They told me they weren't in the business of exploiting my page for money and they put a really solid case forward regarding what they could offer me and where they could see me going in the future.

I was so excited. This was a huge moment. I signed on the dotted line and Sarah became my manager. I felt like a megastar. I HAD A FUCKING MANAGER! I was so gangster. This proved to be the best decision I have ever made, as they were true to their word and supported my growth—including for about eighteen months before I actually started to make any money.

After nearly a decade in commercial radio and with my experience on the 2Day FM breakfast show behind me, I had grown enough of a profile that I was starting to be treated differently at work. I was noticed by management and really valued within the team. I was able to mentor staff, give advice and was trusted to manage important video projects. After about eight months working as a video producer for FoxFM (still in Melbourne), I was offered a shiny new opportunity.

The new gig was on the Carrie and Tommy Show, with the fabulous Carrie Bickmore and the visually pleasing Tommy Little, two of the most divine human beings on this planet. It was the perfect tonic after working on the cut-throat breakfast show: there was no goss, no egos, no fights, nothing. I was treated with real respect and made to feel like an important member of the team. In short, it was an absolute dream. I was excited about the show, the hours suited me a whole lot better than the four am breakfast show starts and I didn't feel constantly stressed or like I was on an inevitable path to quitting in a flurry of tears.

The Carrie and Tommy Show had really found its feet by the end of 2018 and was just a powerhouse. The stuff we were doing was fun and required a lot of focus and attention. By the time the day finished, I would be exhausted. I would get home and just didn't want to do any filming or any work keeping the 'Christian Hull' machine ticking along. I was spent.

It was so much fun, however, I was starting to get busier and busier in my personal life. My videos were getting more and more popular and I was getting heaps of requests for sponsored posts and being offered opportunities I was unable to pursue due to working this demanding full-time job.

I made the decision in March 2019 that I would leave radio forever. I was thankful to be leaving on such a high and so glad I got to spend almost a year working with the amazing people on Carrie and Tommy's show. One of those amazing people was the executive producer, Sonder, who is one of those people who is equally as chaotic as she is genius. She's the definition of a hot mess. You know those people who are so hilarious that you spend most of the day faffing about doing nothing but laughing? That was her. I was really thankful to end my nine years in commercial radio with her. She was that light that you needed and also that person you'd look at and think, 'How on earth have you been put in charge of a national drive show?' But her results spoke for themselves.

Making the decision to leave what I had dedicated the last twelve years of my life to achieving wasn't easy. It all came to a head when I got a phone call from my management, and they told me, 'Christian, all your tour dates have sold out!'

I had decided that I wanted to a big national comedy tour. Sixteen shows in eight cities, with 8000 tickets all up. I KNOW! What an achievement. I am the Taylor Swift of Australia. I was super pumped and extremely proud of selling the tour out. It was going to be a lot of work and I would be on the road each weekend for ten weeks. There was a lot to plan for, a lot of content to perfect and a LOT going on.

I started to feel like I was in over my head. I was feeling super overwhelmed and was worried I wasn't going to be able to both work full-time on Carrie and Tommy's show as well as tour.

This was all surging through my brain one day when I was out to coffee with my close friend Sarah, who I had met working on the 2Day FM breakfast show. I was telling her how nervous I was about juggling the show as a full-time video producer and trying to do a comedy tour, as well as keeping my regular uploads coming.

My biggest concern was that my head wasn't committed to the Carrie and Tommy show one hundred per cent. I loved my job, but I now had this side hustle that was really starting to grow, and I was excited about growing it. I realised that I wasn't going to be able to do both well and I was getting really stressed and anxious about letting down my team.

After I explained this to Sarah, she agreed that there was reason to be concerned about me burning out. She drove me home after the coffee, and in the car on the way home I burst into tears (classic Christian). I just didn't know what I was going to do. I could see myself on a path of total wipe-out. Something had to give. Then Sarah said to me: 'Why don't you resign and do your stuff full-time?'

I don't know why that had never occurred to me—because it was actually the perfect solution to my problems. I realised that the income for the comedy tours I had planned would get me by financially and that for the first time in my life I was financially free to be able to do my own thing. I instantly felt a rush of excitement and later that day I organised a meeting with my boss and set in motion the next step of my life.

Flash forward to now, and I'm at over a million followers, I have completed three sell-out comedy tours and I am making enough money from my own content and performances to live comfortably. Something that started as a hobby has become my ultimate dream come true.

13

THE PERKS OF BEING FAMOUS

Now, at the grand old age of thirty-three, even with the success of my channels, I still don't feel famous—at least not in the way that I thought it would feel when I was a kid. What I have realised is that it's not the fame per se that I have always craved—it was the ability and opportunity to make people feel special and to laugh. I love making videos that cause people to piss themselves. It brings me so much joy. I get so many messages of love and support and I think *that's* what I always wanted. I wanted to feel accepted and adored for my authentic self because as a kid I knew I was different. In the outside world, I was not the star of the show. But in my family I felt like the star and I fucking loved it. I needed to be more than the star behind closed doors.

I grew up watching celebrities looking perfect and photo-shopped, but now there is a whole wave of people making content just being naturally themselves. I'm thankful that I'm here at this time when that content is being created, and when people can pick and choose from a huge variety of entertainment that includes this type of thing. I don't really fit into TV, I don't really fit into radio. The big bosses and management of that traditional media, they don't want this. They don't want the authentic Christian—it's too crass, there's too much dick chat, it's just too vulgar or I'm too full-on, I'm too gay. But discovering YouTube has meant that I can do whatever I want, I can just be myself and I have created an entertainment space that is authentically mine. Nothing is off limits for me—I have shat myself while driving and I will talk about that. I am my true and proper self—I regret nothing I say or film or do. I have no one telling me it is right or wrong, or not 'brand-friendly' or anything like that—I can record whatever I want.

And the most surprising thing of all is that people other than my immediate family actually get it. I get stopped in the street and asked for photos and I love it. I love all the positive comments and love how wonderful people are. It's such a brilliant feeling and a huge ego boost when someone stops me to say that they loved a particular video.

It's not until I leave the bubble of my apartment and travel that I realise how many people have seen my stuff. It's funny because if I thought about it too much, I worry it would limit what I am prepared to make. When I am making my stuff, I am just in the moment. But when I leave the house . . . that's when it all gets real! For example, I was recently in Port Macquarie, and while I was taking a walk on the beach I got stopped by these two young kids who asked to take a snap of me. I posed for the pic and then carried on walking, only to be chased down by these kids who informed me their mother was frantically driving down to the beach to see me and would I mind waiting for two minutes. Karen was her name and it was like we were long-lost friends. She was carrying her 'Trish Bag', a tote bag she had purchased from my online store, and was almost in tears. We had a good ole chat and it was just so rewarding to see the joy on her face. I only wish my own family were that happy to see me.

I'm worried that this sounds arrogant, but it comes from a place where I'm proud of what I've done. I'm so lucky to be in this position. People like Karen have made me the monster I am today. People who watch the videos, buy the book and come to my comedy shows are the people I love. I don't know them personally, but they bring me so much joy. I see their comments even though I suck at replying and I feel like I have a million best friends. I try hard to remain level-headed and keep my feet on the ground, but when I get asked for a photo I fucking die every time. I love it.

It isn't always smooth sailing, though. For example, one unsuspecting normal day in early 2019, I was getting off a plane in Adelaide. By then, I had started to get recognised a bit and it wasn't unusual to have someone approach me and say hi. As I left the plane and walked out into the terminal, I saw a lady whose face just lit up with total excitement the moment she saw me. Being the massive egotist that I am, I beamed at her. She looked just as happy as I felt and she called out, 'It's so great to see you!' I replied, 'It's lovely to meet you' and as I went to hug her, she walked past me with a look of 'who the fuck are you' and hugged someone who was standing right behind me. Someone she actually knew. The someone who was the source of her earlier excitement.

I was mortified and that was the first time I just did a runner. Bolted. How embarrassing and people had watched this unfold too. WHO DID I THINK I WAS!!! Beyoncé? All I know is that the lady in the terminal that day was definitely not ready for this jelly.

The fame thing can have its perks, no doubt about that. Like the time I was cast in a feature film, for example. Now, 'being cast' is a strong statement and possibly a little misleading. It was more like a Facebook message asking if I wanted to play a role in an upcoming Australian movie. The message came from the assistant director of the film, who I had met once at a screening of a TV show she had produced. She had seen my stuff and knew who I was.

The most recent acting gig I'd had was when I was ten and played the role of Vidal Sassoon in some kind of school skit. I was a sassy, gay pre-teen and just had to say the following to the camera: 'The body and shine is utter brilliance, she has the catwalk look, just stunning', as friends of mine walked down a runway. Looking back at it now, it was some fucking weird project about body image that was put on, if memory serves me correctly, at a large international teacher's conference. We were then interviewed about how we perceived ourselves. All the kids were asked what's one thing they would change about themselves. When it got to me, I was so happy with myself that I didn't know what to say, so I panicked and just said I hated my nose. I had the cutest little dainty nose at ten—what was I thinking! I should have just owned being the little confident fuck I was and said nothing!

Which is all to say that when I received this Facebook message asking me to be in a film, having pretty much no training and zero acting ability, I responded saying I would be very keen but that I should probably be auditioned. The assistant director phoned me and said that an audition wouldn't be necessary. She also mentioned that the director of the film was Rachel Griffiths.

SORRY?

Rachel fucking Griffiths, Australian acting royalty. Rachel is a fan of my stuff too, the assistant director then told me. I was just about on the floor, half having a heart attack, half planning what to say when I won the Oscar. She then just casually dropped into the conversation that Sam Neill was in the film too. Just an FYI: *Jurassic Park* is one of my favourite films of all time.

It was at this point that I absolutely insisted on an audition—I didn't want to get the role of a lifetime only to be shunned from the acting community because I wasn't ready. I googled acting classes and briefly considered flying to Sydney to take some emergency classes at NIDA.

But I said yes, and the assistant director hooked me up with the casting people, who told me I would be playing a nurse. I was losing my mind. I was born for this role. Obviously, it was a comedy—why else would they want me?

A few days later, I got an email informing me that my role would only require a one-day shoot. That was okay, I reassured myself, I could cope with a best supporting actor Oscar. Hell, Viola Davis won an Oscar for her role in the movie *Doubt* and she only had eight minutes of screen time. I had this. My speech was all ready to go and I hadn't even seen the script. Looking back, one might say that I got a tad ahead of myself.

The email from the casting team went into further detail about the film, and as I read it I realised the movie was actually a very serious biopic about Michelle Payne, Australia's first female jockey to win the Melbourne Cup. Her story is unbelievable—perfect for a movie. I became even more excited!

On the ascribed day, I headed into the studios to meet with the costume team and to get the script. I got fitted for my scrubs, collected my two lines and returned home to rehearse them. TWO LINES! Not much, but I was going to own those two lines. I was going to get my face on screen and deliver these lines like no other. YOU CAN'T HANDLE THE TRUTH!

I'm not going to lie: I was a little puzzled by the scene. It was quite a sad moment in the movie. Michelle's father is in hospital and is going to die, I am the nurse on duty and the entire Payne family is sitting in the hospital room looking super sad. I walk in and tell them visiting hours are over and to go home. It couldn't have been clearer that I had *not* been given the tap due to my comedy skills. This was a serious scene for a serious actor. But I had this, I told myself. Again.

The experience of filming my scene was incredible. The whole cast was there: Teresa Palmer and Sam Neill were two feet from me and I also shared the scene with Brooke Satchwell, who I have loved forever. It was daunting but unreal.

The scene was being filmed in a hospital in Bundoora just outside of Melbourne and the day had run over time, so we were late to film my scene. The hospital would only let us film until five-thirty pm and it was already five pm so I had to do my scene pronto and make way for a few more final scenes to be shot before they wrapped for the day.

The pressure was on. I was given my mark and Rachel gave me a pep talk and then she left the room. There was a crew of about twelve on cameras and audio, there were the assistant directors and the entire cast was watching me. A room full of professionals, then me! Some guy who wears wigs and makes shitty videos.

'ACTION!'

I walked over to Sam Neill and Teresa Palmer and delivered my lines.

'CUT!'

Rachel came bounding out of nowhere, pulled me aside, told me that she loved it, gave me a bit of direction on how she wanted the line delivered, gave me another pep talk and then bounded back into her seat and screamed 'ACTION!' again.

This process repeated for about six takes and I was starting to feel like an absolute failure. The cast and crew couldn't have been nicer, but I just felt like I was fucking woeful. We changed angles and I did the line a bunch more times.

By the end of the whole humiliating experience, I was convinced that my scene would just be cut. However, I knew it was actually a crucial part of the story. I wondered whether they would just have to find a way to make my shitty acting work.

Nine months passed.

Then one day I got a call that they wanted me to come back into their audio studios to dub in my lines. This is a standard practice and got me excited because it meant I was in the film! I rocked up at the studios and was ushered into an audio booth. My scene was going to be played on a screen and I just had to say my lines again.

I was about to see my big moment. About to see my face on the big screen for the first time. This was insane. I was going to be in a film with some amazing names. They played me the scene and I was so excited and nervous, just waiting to see my face flash up and deliver an Oscar-winning performance.

One of the assistant directors said, 'Okay, so that's your scene. We just want you to deliver the lines, you can ad lib a bit too.'

Wait, hang on. That was my scene? I didn't see me in it.

They gave me a cue and then my scene played again. As I was watching the scene again, desperately scanning it for my reflection, I realised that they had pretty much just cut around me and edited the scene, so I didn't appear in it at all.

There is a wonderful close-up of the fat rolls on the back of my head and that's it.

So, that's my debut feature film. I was Mike Wazowski'd.

I was invited to the premiere and it was a big deal. It was a packed theatre, the entire Payne family was there and it was very emotional. When my scene came on, I was so excited and felt like I was actually going to be nominated for at least an AACTA Award. It was good.

The film is called *Ride Like a Girl* and if you want to see my bit, it's right towards the end. I'll just be here in the corner, crying with excitement! I AM IN A FILM (for two seconds and it's the back of my head).

Part Four

THE SEALED
SECTION

14

LITTLE NAPKIN, BIG SECRET

When people first meet me, they know I'm gay before I walk in the door. I am very thankful that you can just tell I am gay. It makes life so much easier. It meant I didn't need to come out. Mum and Dad just knew, they were eased into my gayness slowly over the years and it didn't hit them for six.

I JUST GOT A SPORTING REFERENCE IN! The publisher wanted me to appeal to blokes, so this should do it. I mean, let's be real—this entire chapter is about me appealing to blokes: a-peeling their clothes off, that is. Bit of humour.

I never told my parents I was gay, I just didn't need to. You don't need to tell your parents that you're straight and I didn't have to tell mine that I was gay.

There was one time that Mum tried to get it out of me. I remember it so clearly and at the time I was horrified and embarrassed. Not because I was gay, but because talking about anything to do with sex with Mum was gross.

I was in my room, in bed watching TV. I had the door closed. I was in Year Twelve at the time, it was my final year of high school. The show I was watching was ABC-TV's *Australian Story* and it was about a young boy going through Year Twelve and also battling depression and having to deal with being gay. It didn't end well—he took his own life. It was so incredibly sad.

I knew Mum and Dad were watching the same show out in the TV room because I could hear it on out there too. When the show finished, I heard their TV go off and I just knew Mum was coming in to talk and make sure I was okay. She is such a good mum. I knew what was about to happen and I knew it was going to be super awkward.

I decided to pretend to be asleep to avoid the conversation. I didn't want to have it. However, my TV was still on, and I knew that as soon as Mum walked in she would see I had been watching the same show. I grabbed a shoe and threw it at the TV in the hope that it would turn off. It didn't, but to my relief it did change the channel.

Mum walked in and sat on the end of my bed. I pretended to be super tired—I even put on the world's worst tired voice and told her I just needed to sleep. But she wouldn't leave. Bloody Mum. She then asked if I had seen any of the show.

Of course I said no, and told her that I had no idea what she was talking about.

I looked at my TV and saw that the channel it had changed to was SBS and there was a documentary on about pasteurising milk. It could have been much worse, right! Imagine if it had been *Queer As Folk*, with a hardcore sex scene. HOW WOULD THAT CONVERSATION HAVE GONE!

'I have no idea what show you are talking about, Mum,' I said coolly. 'I have been glued to this documentary about milk pasteurisation for the last hour, it's so fascinating.' Highly believable. Some of my best work, really.

In true Mum style, this did not put her off and she proceeded to tell me about the show she'd just watched and the young boy and everything he went through. She then asked if I was okay and whether I needed to talk to her about anything.

I wanted to die. I pulled the blankets over my head and said I was so tired I just needed to go to sleep. Poor Mum. She turned my TV off and left. 'MUM, I WAS WATCHING THAT!' I never did find out how to properly pasteurise milk. I could google it, but . . . BUSY BUSY!

I knew she knew. But she waited until I was really ready to accept who I was. She is a good egg.

Dad was also amazing—he gave no shits whatsoever. The first time it ever came up in conversation was the year I volunteered at Mardi Gras (a huge gay pride parade that happens each year in Sydney—it's massive and basically Gay

Christmas) when I was about twenty-two. He told me to make sure to use a condom if I had sex. I was still a virgin at the time, as I totally wasn't confident enough to have sex at that point. But bless him! He believed in me!

The first person I actually came right out and told was my best friend Ashleigh. I was eighteen, maybe nineteen, we had finished school and we were at West Ryde RSL. West Ryde RSL was where retirees and families went to eat and play bingo. There was always a cover band playing in one of the theatres, and I think that particular day it was the Bee Gees. Totally irrelevant fact, but I need to set the scene and the scene is old people for whom 'Stayin' Alive' is less a fun retro dance track and more of a genuine plea.

That night, I had picked up Ash from her parents' place and had driven us both to the RSL for a cheap feed and a catch-up (not for the aforementioned Bee Gees cover band). We lined up and ordered our dinner. You order numbers, not actual dishes, and I got number 34 (sweet and sour pork) and Ashleigh got number 12 (satay chicken). We took our pager and sat down at a little round table.

I had invited Ash out for dinner with the sole purpose of telling her the shocking news that she definitely had no idea about, that ... wait for it ... I'M GAY! I had imagined that she would be so stunned by this news that she would spit her drink out all over our dinner, stand up, flip the table and storm out in a fit of rage. 'BUT I'M IN LOVE WITH YOU!' she would scream as she exited hastily.

I had imagined this scenario despite the fact that at no point in our friendship had Ash or I ever had romantic or sexual feelings for each other. The thought of being romantically involved with her makes me feel awkward. I know she feels the same way about me. This is one of the reasons we had been able to become so close—neither of us had ulterior motives. But why let the truth get in the way of a highly dramatic, if imagined, scene?

We sat down and were chatting away as usual. I was so nervous. I decided that I would wait until after dinner to tell her. I didn't want us to have to sit in silence and finish a meal if the conversation went badly. So I said nothing. We continued talking away but I wasn't listening to a word she was saying—I was nodding and oohing and ahhing in all the right places, but what I was actually doing was practising my lines in my head. I only had two words in the script ('I'm gay!'), but I was running through all of the possible reactions Ash might have. I was also questioning whether my choice of sweet and sour pork was going to be enough, and wondering if I should have got number 18 (Mongolian lamb) as well, with fried rice. I am a big eater.

Our pager pinged and I collected our number 12 and number 34 from the pass. Thankfully, they were enormous servings and came with a mountain of complimentary prawn crackers. We ate in companionable silence. After we'd finished, Ash got up to go to the bathroom, and while she was gone I scribbled the words 'I'm gay' on a spare napkin. I was going to hand it to her when she got back. Wasn't that the stupidest plan ever? What if she just thought she had some satay sauce on her face and missed the 'secret message' altogether?

But when she came back, I couldn't go through with it. Even though deep down I was pretty sure she would be totally fine with my revelation, there was still a small part of me that couldn't be one hundred per cent sure. I guess my fear came down to the fact that she was my closest friend and the only real friend who I felt comfortable with at the time. There was a lot at stake for me: if I lost Ash as a friend, I would literally have no other close friends. None.

Don't get me wrong—I have a lot of beautiful friendships and I adore a lot of people (special mention to Chantelle and Belinda, who will be reading this and be so cut if I don't mention them). But Ashleigh and I are next-level close. We have a bond I don't think I'll ever have with anyone else.

As I went to hand Ashleigh the little napkin with my big secret on it, I remembered that I had to drop her home. DAMN IT! I didn't want the car ride to be awkward, so I decided to wait until we got to her house. Sitting in the car out the front of her house, I told her that I was going to hand her a note on a napkin and that she was only allowed to read it once I had driven away.

This would be such an amazing end to a movie. The scene would go like this: Ashleigh gets out of the car, closes the door and watches as I drive off. Cut to me, in the driver's seat, looking in the rear-vision mirror and seeing her open the napkin. Cut to an over-the-shoulder shot of her reading the napkin and you can see me driving away in the distance. Fade to black! Credits roll. Oh my god, what an ending. (Plus, ripe for a sequel—I'm no fool!) I'd finally get my face on the big screen and not just the back of my head.

It pretty much went exactly like that and I got a text from her saying something nice and that was that. To think I had almost let the stress of it put me off my meal. It was a total anticlimax. But I was so relieved and so glad I had finally told someone. It was the first step in understanding who I was and what I was going to be. A gay!

Also, it is worth mentioning that a few years later Ashleigh came out to me! FUCKING BULLSHIT! I am the only gay in the village. I am different and special, not you as well! It's fair to say that the table-flipping, storming-out scene I had imagined taking place in West Ryde RSL eventually did have its day. When she revealed her revolting secret to me, I screamed in her face and told her she was disgusting. Lesbian! So gross. Of course, I followed that with a hug! But I was in shock—how had I not seen it? Maybe it was because I am so self-absorbed. Whatever, mainly I was excited to be in a power gay-couple relationship.

I have a very close relationship with both of my parents, but it took a good while to develop this closeness. I was pretty closed off from them in high school. These were the years when I was super awkward and didn't really have any friends, so when Mum would ask me about my day, I didn't want to talk about it because I didn't want her to know that I had no friends and spent my lunchtimes in the library by myself.

Looking back now, I wish I'd been more open with them throughout those years—they were so supportive and always had my best interests at heart. I wish I could say that once I left school and got a full-time job, I changed. But, honestly, I think I got worse.

It wasn't until I moved out of home and to Newcastle that my relationship with Mum and Dad really blossomed. Having to do everything on my own without them there as a safety net really brought home to me how much they'd done for me over the years and how ungrateful I had always been. In Newcastle, my confidence also started to grow and I started behaving out in the world in a way that more closely reflected who I had always been with my family. I suppose I came to the realisation that Mum and Dad had always supported who I was and how I decided to live my life, and not only had they supported me, but they really, really loved me. In the end, it is their love and acceptance that has enabled me to be my authentic self.

Like I said earlier, I didn't ever officially 'come out' to the parentals. I didn't need to. It just kind of happened organic- ally. It turns out that Mum had been pretty sure I was gay from when I was in Year Ten. She'd noticed that I had lots of platonic female friends and hardly any male friends and she'd also been picking up on my gay aesthetic since I was a child—apparently, I used to compliment my kindergarten teacher on her outfits! It was more of a dawning realisation thing rather than a lightning bolt moment for Dad too. As far as he was concerned, it was not a big deal. His work with Qantas had exposed him to a lot of gay men, so there was nothing shocking or even mysterious about being gay to him.

Mum and Dad had the usual cool parents' response of not judging me because of my sexuality, but of harbouring some worry that it would make my life harder than it otherwise would have been. They worried about me finding a suitable life partner and achieving my dreams, but as they have said, they had the same worries for my three brothers, who are all straight. And while they will admit that they sometimes thought being gay was a harder road than being straight, they also believed in me, knew I was strong and were sure that I would be okay.

As for my brothers, well that's an even more ridiculous story. Not only did I not have to come out to them, but I don't think we have ever even really discussed it deeply to this day—and not because we are awkwardly avoiding the subject, but just because it is no big deal. I support them and they support me: it is that simple and always has been.

There have been a few laughs along the way, though. One night when I was about twenty-one—so the triplets would have been sixteen or seventeen—the whole family was sitting around the dinner table and we were all in a passionate discussion about something. My family is loud and Mum, Nick, Tim and I constantly talk over the top of each other while my father and Adrian just sit there and watch the chaos—occasionally trying to get a word in when they can.

It was common knowledge among my family that I was 'a gay', but at that point it hadn't really been confirmed officially. Nick was bitching about a teacher at his school who had told Nick he had to do something that Nick didn't want to do. He was mid-whinge when he came out with the following: 'I'm just so annoyed. Why do I have to do it? It's so gaaaaaaaaaaaaaaa . . .'

He had been going to say, 'It's so gay.' But he had realised that what he was about to blurt out was actually a put-down and was not the right thing to say, especially in front of me. And what he did next to save himself was so awkward and funny. He drew out the first half of the word: 'Gaaaaaaaaaaaaaaa . . .' and then mid-word he quickly changed what he was going to say: 'Gaaaaaaaaaaaaaaa-rate. It's so great!'

I instantly knew what he was doing, and I thought it was a really nice, if awkward, moment. I knew he knew I was gay, and I also knew he was okay with it. It was a weird abrupt sentence that made no sense in the end. I laughed and we all carried on with the conversation.

I look back at my situation and know that I am so lucky to have the family that I do. It's not always that easy to come out. I have heard stories of people being kicked out of home, ignored and totally abandoned by their family. I was lucky to have parents who were so open-minded and had experienced life to its fullest. I think having older parents who had worked in the fashion and airline industries helped.

I often wonder why or how a parent can just close off and kick their child out for something that's not a choice. As I get older, I have come to realise that often religion plays a strong hand. A person's upbringing and their generation have a role in it too. I guess what I have learned from people's stories is that when you are brought up and told time and time again that being gay is a sin and will send you to hell, in the end you just believe it.

Thankfully, these days I am seeing so much more love and acceptance from parents, kids and families, as I think we have realised as a society, in Australia anyway, that it is okay to be gay. And if my out-and-proud presence on Facebook and YouTube plays even a tiny role in mainstreaming that message, then that actually means the world to me.

15

THE SEX FILES

I don't have a sex addiction, but when I tell people my 'number', their eyes widen and they look horrified. I think I use sex as a way to feel good about myself. I hate my body and I hate how I look, so for me hooking up is a way of telling myself that I'm not gross and I am attractive to some people.

My relationship with sex started the way it does for most teenage boys: with perving and masturbating. For me, I couldn't get enough of naked male bodies . . . especially of 'D'. One fairly easy way of me getting to see dick as a teen was by watching a show that some people might remember quite well.

Big Brother was a TV show where a bunch of random people would go into a house and live together with viewers voting to evict one person a week until there was a winner. Now, for those of you who are the same age as me, you would also remember *Big Brother Uncut*. This was uncensored footage of the housemates showing their dicks and being naughty. As a teenager with no access to the internet, it was my version of porn. We all remember Dean! Well, I certainly do. [insert eggplant emoji]

Big Brother Uncut was on at ten-thirty on a Thursday night (I love that the time and day is burnt into my brain). I never missed one episode. Every Thursday, I would sneak into the living room after everyone had gone to bed and watch the entire show. Unfortunately for me, our family holidays to the Blue Mountains sometimes took place around the same time of year that *Big Brother* was on TV. But I wasn't going to let the Blue Mountains get in the way of seeing peen. If there's a peen to be seen, I am the queen of seeing the peen. Poetry in motion.

One fateful Thursday night in the mountains, with my cousins and brothers tucked up in their beds and my parents and aunt and uncle safely retired to their rooms, I did my usual trick of slipping silently out of my bed, creeping downstairs and switching the TV on to tune into the uncut feast of nudity and dick that I so needed. In order to hear the TV without waking anyone up and being sprung, I would set the volume on one (let's face it, I was primarily here for the visuals) and then I would sit one inch away from the screen in order to hear what was going on.

This night, it was about eleven pm and I had got through the first half hour. No peen action yet. The host, Gretel Killeen, was (and remains) my hero—I loved her, she was so sassy and witty. She threw to an ad break and hinted that up next was shower time. Guaranteed nudity was on the way!

The show resumed after the commercial break and it was time for the nude shower scene! I was so ready to see peen. Suddenly—*BAM!*—there were boobs and vag on the TV. Gross! Get off the screen, hurry up and cut to Marty (he was hot)!

'Christian, turn that off and go to bed.'

I was so invested in the promise of upcoming penis, I had failed to hear Mum approaching. Faster than you can imagine, I turned the TV off. I sat there, feeling awkward.

Oh the horror. I thought it was the end of the world—I'd been caught trying to see dick. My life was over. The jig was up. Mum now knew everything. But for Mum, of course, it was nothing too serious—just a curious teenager looking at some boobs. But for me, it was a devastating loss: I'd invested thirty minutes in the show and then right before they were going to cut to a giant cock, I was caught red-handed one inch from the TV screen.

Before I could apologise, Mum had turned around and headed back to bed so, naturally, I turned the TV back on and caught a glimpse of some D. Success. Nowadays, kids have it so easy. This went on to be a recurring theme in my life story. Trying desperately to catch a glimpse of the D any way I could. I had no shame. I am also pleased to say this continues to be my life story.

I would, however, like to clarify a few things about my sex life. My campy nature means that people think I'm a 'power bottom', meaning I only take it up the butt and refuse to give it. I only wish this were the case—because that would mean I could just lie there and have the other guy do all the work. The dream.

Sadly, this isn't the case.

I don't do anal. It is too painful: the anus is an exit hole, not an entry hole, and not designed to have something thrust into it, thank you very much. I also don't often give anal either. But frankly, that's less for philosophical reasons and more due to the fact that I don't have the fitness level to thrust for three to five minutes. Sex is so exhausting.

When I tell people this, I inevitably get asked, 'Well, what the hell *do* you do?' This response generally only comes from straight men (surprise, surprise!). Straight men don't realise that there is in fact a lot more to sex than sticking your penis inside something. I feel sorry for their partners. I really do.

I admit it: there were multiple times in my early twenties when I would drive out to a carpark at night to meet up with a guy and do things in the backseat with him. This was in my thinner, more flexible days, and while it was kinda hot having someone insert themselves into you, it never really got me going. I have been penetrated a few times but have never enjoyed it.

However, I think the reason why I refuse and will always refuse comes down to one particular incident that took place one night in a park in Epping. I'd met up with this guy and we had planned to just do a few things, nothing too full-on . . . except he had other plans. There we were, making out and having a good time. It wasn't long before we began to remove our clothes and then, just as I was thinking what a great time we were having, he just shoved it in.

WITHOUT WARNING.

DRY.

Holy mother of god! Why would you do that?!

It was the single most painful sexual experience I have ever had—and that's saying a lot, as I once actually ripped my dick during sexy time. He literally tore me a new asshole— when most people use that saying, it's metaphorical. Not this guy!

I was so angry. After I cried out so loudly that I almost woke greater Epping and its surrounds, he said sorry, spat on his hand and offered to prepare the area.

It's a NO from me, kind sir. I left and from that moment have never had a dick up the butt again.

I hope my family enjoyed reading this chapter!

16

THE DAILY GRIND(R)

For a long time, I thought I was a sex addict. How hilarious is that—it turns out I was just a man! Horny all the time. I didn't lose my virginity until I was twenty-three, so from the age of twenty-three to twenty-eight, I one hundred per cent made up for lost time. I worked myself around to literally anyone. (Worked = whored for free.)

At twenty-three, I was still living at home so that made pursuing sex at every available opportunity more difficult, but I am not one to give up easily. On the odd occasion, I would sneak guys through the side gate and into the tiny spare bedroom downstairs and we would do our thing on a single bed usually reserved for visiting relatives. That's right, Aunty Susie, you were sleeping in my sex room.

I would say I am a little sex-pesty. When I'm not filming or editing videos or ordering or eating Uber Eats, you can guarantee I'll be on Grindr. There is a feature on my phone that allows me to see how much time I spend on various apps. The third on my list is Grindr and I have been known to spend upwards of an hour a day on it. That tells you I am a desperate whore in need of attention.

Grindr, for those who are unaware, is an app for the gays that basically tells you who is thirsty for sex. It lists all the thirst men in order of who is geographically closest to you. You log on and then search to your heart's content for someone to cross swords with. Now, apparently some gays use Grindr to find friends and create meaningful connections—I call absolute bullshit on this. Grindr is not an app to find friends. It's an app for your dick.

I have been using the app for years and my success rate is, at best, mediocre. If you log on to the app, it's a sea of guns, abs and eye candy. This means I have had to be very smart in how I advertise myself—high angles and Vaseline on the lens are my friends. Taking the perfect nude pic is also an acquired skill that so many guys fail at.

Here are some of my tips for nude pics on Grindr:

1. High angles: this tends to make you look better and make the right things look bigger.
2. No one wants to see a pic taken from underneath your dick looking back up at your gut and double chin.

3. The only time to send a close-up photo of your anus is when it's specifically requested.

4. Variety is the spice of life: dick close-up, full body nude, erect dick, flaccid dick, dick in hand, the list goes on. No one wants the same close-up of your dick sixteen times—that's not enticing, that's time-wasting. You need to send the full range of what we can expect.

5. And I cannot say this strongly enough: up-to-date photos.

If you follow these tips, you will avoid awkward encounters and disappointments. Of course, I learned all of this the hard way. I have had a few guys rock up to my place and, due to my old nudes, I wasn't what I once was. Let me tell you: it's unfair on them and so embarrassing and shameful for me.

Looking back, though, it's pretty funny how some of these encounters played out. Here are just two of the highlights. Encounter number one: guy comes to front door, Christian opens front door, guy looks Christian up and down, guy says he left his phone in the car and leaves. Guy does not return. Encounter number two: guy makes it to Christian's bedroom, Christian notices panic on guy's face, guy says he doesn't have much time to fool around, Christian realises guy is trying desperately to find a way out of hook-up, Christian offers lifeline by telling guy he can come back at a later date, guy accepts offer and flees the scene. Guy does not return at a later date. Guy blocks Christian on Grindr.

I am not bothered by these at all—actually, I totally get it. After a few experiences like this, which left me feeling like shit about myself, I decided that it was time to maybe use photos of my true self, not just those taken from the highest angles imaginable. There's no point in lying, or even stretching the truth really, because all you'll do is land yourself in these types of situations. Horny and alone. Which, coincidently, is my Grindr bio.

And it goes both ways. I have had my fair share of guys rocking up to my place who were nothing like their pics. One memorable time, I saw a cute guy online and not far from me, so I messaged him and got a reply. He sent some pics and we discussed what we would do to each other. So I invited him over.

I got a knock on the door and opened it to find my older neighbour, presumably popping over to ask for a cup of sugar or whatever the fuck it was that neighbours did for each other in the olden days. We said hi, there was an awkward pause and then I realised this wasn't my older neighbour, it was the guy I'd invited over. He was after sugar, all right, but not the kind a neighbour wants for baking. It turned out the pics he had sent me were from when he was twenty years old, from way back in 1978. NINETEEN SEVENTY-EIGHT, my friends! I had just assumed it was a filter, but on later inspection I could see that it was a pic of a pic. He was pretty hot, so I hadn't questioned it.

Here is a tip: always, *always*, question it. If it seems too good to be true, it usually is!

I hate confrontation so badly that I didn't say anything and just went through with it. What can I say? My mother taught me to be polite to my elders. It wasn't bad, but it wasn't at all what I was looking for. But can you believe that my fear of confrontation is so bad that I ended up sleeping with a sixty-year-old because I was too scared to tell him he was too old for me?! I would like to say that I learned a valuable lesson that day. But I didn't and this mistaken identity routine happened a few more times with different guys. Sometimes, it was a photo of someone who was very fit and they would rock up and they were not quite as fit . . . Sometimes it wasn't even a photo of them. I was catfished quite a bit.

I have had many a guy send pics of himself from better days. I have learned over the years to really become a stalker and track down people's Instagram profiles to make sure they are who they say. I am picky about who I invite over, and I know to look at me you might think 'beggars can't be choosers', but we can be and I am.

I did have a few very successful earlier experiences with Grindr. And some extremely unsuccessful ones. And some that started out GREAT and then turned into a nightmare. I am about to tell you about one of the latter.

While still living at home, I would sneak out and meet up with this really hot guy and we would fool around in my car. He was next-level hot. We'd recline the front seat so that it was flat, I would lie back and he would just climb on top.

One night, while he was on top of me, his body pressed against mine—we were always fully naked—he slid down a little and, how do I say this delicately, as he slid his body, down with it went my foreskin (yes, mine is intact) and he kept sliding and so did everything else and then it ripped off.

Let me explain.

There are two points on the penis where the foreskin is attached: what happened to me was that as old mate slid down me, my poor foreskin got caught up in the friction of our skin contact, was dragged down and one of these attachments tore. Just google 'banjo string' if you need it further explained.

The pain was bad but, being a sex addict, I pushed through the pain and said nothing. It was very dark so I thought I could get away with it. Then the pain got really intense and we had to stop. That's when I realised there was blood absolutely fucking everywhere.

When I saw what had happened, naturally, I freaked out. But I didn't want him to feel bad or freak out, so I brushed it off as nothing. I also wanted to see him again, so I didn't want to be a total weirdo and start crying. I dropped him home and then I headed back to my place and had a shower.

Jesus Christ! The pain of the water was so horrible. Everything hurt. I thought my dick was going to fall off. For the next few weeks, I left it alone. (That period of time is still my PB in terms of letting my D just be.) Peeing was a bit stingy. All is well now, however. It is still a bit tender in places but fully functional.

This has been a public health announcement, authorised by C Hull of the Grindr Party, Australia.

Living at home meant I had to answer to my parents, which in turn made sneaking out for Grindr hook-ups difficult— actually, nearly fucking impossible. The front door was loud and the side door was right near the TV, so secretly leaving the house while Mum and Dad were still up wasn't an option. I would finish dinner and retreat to my room, then I would jump on to Grindr and search for someone. Generally, once you found someone, you would arrange to meet. If they could host—awesome! But if they couldn't, not so awesome. Luckily, I had a car, which was also a sex palace.

The next step was getting out of the house. My usual plan was just to very confidently leave—I'd run the gauntlet trying to get out of the house as quickly as possible before Mum and Dad had time to yell 'Where the heck you goin' at this time of night, boy?' (for some reason, in this story, my parents are played by hillbillies with southern US accents). Nine times out of ten, I would get caught and would have to come up with an excuse as to why I was leaving the house at nine-thirty pm.

'Where are you off to?'

I had three mainstays that I would crack out at this juncture:

1. 'To the shops!'
2. 'To see Ashleigh!'
3. 'To see Chantelle!'

These were my go-to answers. But Mum and Dad weren't done yet, and would often hit me with a goddamn follow-up question:

'Why?'

I had to dig deep at this point, but some of my most successful responses included:

1. 'I need to get a face mask.'
2. 'To return a book.'
3. 'Just for a catch up.'

Having to go through these motions and make this shit up would anger me so much. I was twenty-three, still living at home and leaving at nine-thirty pm. What the fuck did they think I was doing? It was so obvious I was going out for sex, because five minutes later I would be home again. I would return home empty-handed with no face mask from the shops and clearly I hadn't been catching up with Ashleigh as she lived twenty minutes away! When I did get home with my clothes on backwards and my hair all over the place, Dad would then routinely ask me: 'How is Ashleigh?'

Dad, how dumb are you? I was clearly out having sex. There was one point I wanted to ask them if they could please stop asking me where I was going. I got really close to just putting it out there and saying, 'I'm trying to sneak out for sex, but you keep grilling me with 900 questions! Can't a guy go and jizz in peace!'

But I never said anything. I just hoped that they would get the picture. They never did, then I moved out of home.

17

NEWCASTLE NIGHTS

I have been on Grindr since 2011 and I am an absolute pro on it. I am the real deal and I know how the whole thing works and nothing can shock me—if there were blue ticks on Grindr, I would definitely have one. However, it wasn't always the case and, in the early days, I used to be terrified about random guys coming over. I would hide a knife under the bed, just in case.

The only time I was genuinely scared was when I lived in Newcastle. Newcastle was my extreme whore phase—I would do anything that moved and got a little experimental. Nothing extreme, just the odd group encounter or venturing out into a park at night.

One day, I invited over a guy and he brought a friend along without letting me know. I hadn't been doing the sex thing for long, so I was still a little shy and sheltered. I had never been more scared because these two guys looked like gang-sters—tattoos and singlets and very muscly. They pretty much just told me what to do the entire time. I was too scared to say anything until they asked me to start talking dirty to them. I had never done this before. But I quickly learned that although these two guys were tough units, they liked someone to treat them a little rough. Just imagine little Christian (I was a lot slimmer back then) telling these guys in an aggressive tone that they were 'dirty boys'. I was so unconvincing because I was just so scared of them. I tried my best to humiliate them by yelling quite full-on profanities at them, but they kept telling me to slap them and I was just like, WHAT HAVE I GOT MYSELF INTO?!

THEN THIS HAPPENED!

They told me to take a sniff of this stuff they'd brought with them, they said it would help me go wild. The two of them had been sniffing away at it since they'd arrived. They handed me a small jar of liquid and told me to block one nostril and inhale the fumes. I was a little nervous but thought, fuck it, I'll just do it, it can't be that bad. As soon as I sniffed, I became a different person. I screamed at one of them and then slapped him really hard on the ass. I felt as though nothing worried me and became Whorella de Vil!

This was my introduction to what's known as amyl. It's a substance that people (mostly gays) inhale to really get in the mood. It gives you an instant rush and then you just turn into a sexual deviant. It doesn't last long, so you usually see guys go hell for leather on the stuff. I guess it must be super addictive, as sometimes I'll hook up with a guy who pretty much needs it to finish.

But after my amyl experience, I got one of the worst headaches of my life! It was so painful. I have used the stuff a few times since but the headaches are just far too severe, so these days when I get offered it, I pass.

Newcastle was the first place I lived after moving out of home (if you discount the three disastrous weeks I spent in Young). After commuting from Sydney for a few months, I took the plunge and made the move. I moved in with someone, who out of respect I will only say wasn't the greatest flatmate in the world—lovely but very messy. We lived just near Merewether Beach. I didn't really like being in the house, so when I got home from work at around ten pm I would go for a walk along the beach. This became a nightly routine and I ended up losing about seven kilograms because of it. The sound of the water was so soothing and the track I would walk along was paved and well-lit, so I felt really safe.

I quickly discovered that at night the crowd of people who walked along this path weren't all health nuts and fitness gurus, nor were they drug dealers or thugs. They were, in fact, mostly guys looking for something a little extra. I worked this out when I noticed two guys who'd been walking in totally separate directions stop and then instantly turn around and go off into the bushes. At first, I was like, 'That's weird, are they doing an illegal deal?' I wanted to go and be nosy, see what they were up to, but I couldn't work up the nerve for fear of getting knifed and left for dead.

A few nights later, I saw something super similar happen and after that I just *kept* seeing guys wandering off together. One night, I noticed two guys walk into a nearby public bathroom. I gave them a little head start and then crept in to see what was happening. I had my suspicions—I was pretty sure they were having sexy times—but I just wanted to check. *BAM!* Sure enough, they were doing some questionable things . . . and they weren't even trying to hide it—I basically walked in on them. I was like a deer in headlights, just staring at them like a creep and not moving. They looked at me and I looked at them. SHIT! What do I do now? I hadn't planned to actually walk in on them naked! So I did what any gay would do—I offered assistance. And they were happy to accept a helping hand.

It turned out this particular stretch of beach path where I had been innocently walking for weeks was actually a hotspot of naughty sexy times—a 'gay beat', to use the vernacular. Just an added bonus on my nightly walks. Let's just say, once I knew this, I may have participated in a few off-path activities myself. To be honest, it would have felt rude not to: you can't just walk through a beat every night and keep an arm's length—that'd be perverted as fuck.

One particularly notable time, I ended up hooking up with a 'straight' guy who was just trying to enjoy a beer, but I gravely misread his signals. I was heading home from one of my nightly beach strolls and I noticed a guy sitting alone on one of the benches. I stopped and stood at a nearby fence, looking out into the nothingness of the ocean and waiting to see if he would do anything—like approach me. He was probably in his mid-twenties and hot, hence why instead of going home I decided to see if this guy was up for a bit of [eggplant emoji]. I stood looking out into the ocean for ages but he didn't move.

Then finally he got up and walked off. Well, that was a complete waste of twenty minutes! I sat down on the bench he'd vacated and opened Grindr to see if he was on it. Disappointingly, he wasn't, so I spent another twenty minutes scrolling to see who else was around. As I was about to get up and walk off, he reappeared out of nowhere and sat down beside me. I thought to myself: this is so on! We talked for a while about random stuff. He told me that he was from out of town and was staying in the pub across the road. I couldn't work him out. He was giving no signals and the conversation was dragging on. I thought I'd just get the ball rolling and go for it. I said to him, 'Shall we go for a walk over here?' I was extremely unsubtle about what I wanted, and I was sure he would just be like, 'I thought you'd never ask.' Well, that's not what happened at all.

Instead, he asked 'Why?' in a really puzzled tone. I was like, 'No reason, I just thought we could go for a walk.' He looked at me really funny and asked if I was okay. I was in sheer panic mode by then and seriously contemplated just bolting. He explained to me he had been watching me looking out to the sea and had come back to talk to me on the bench because he'd thought I was sad and lonely and that I was about to just end it all by walking into the water. He said he thought I was contemplating my life while I was staring into the ocean. He didn't realise I was just horny and that I'd thought he was wanting some fun. We'd got our signals very mixed up. To be fair, horny and alone does look pretty similar to sad and alone.

I explained to him that this particular area was actually a spot where guys come to meet up with other guys and do naughty things and that I had thought he was wanting something a little different. He was pretty surprised and assured me he wasn't, but suddenly became curious about the goings-on of the area. I answered his questions as best I could, and then I just wanted to go home so I got up to leave. But he kept talking to me and asking me more questions. Finally, I politely said goodbye and as I went to leave *for the third time*, he just flat out asked me back to his hotel room.

SHUT THE FRONT DOOR!

He assured me he wasn't gay and repeatedly told me he had slept with many girls. We went back to his hotel room and he turned all the lights off so it was pitch black, and then the magic happened.

And by 'magic', I mean thirty seconds later he finished and then had a mild freak-out and told me (again) that he wasn't gay. I mean, he obviously enjoyed himself—thirty seconds was a bit of a record. I went on home, smiling to myself and wondering whether this was how Jehovah's Witnesses felt when they converted someone. Had I lured him over to the dark side?

I lived in Newcastle for almost four years. After the share-house, I moved to a small, one-bedroom treehouse—a cosy little place on stilts nestled on the side of a super steep hill. I was just loving myself and loving this chance I had to explore. Having my own above-ground sex dungeon was amazing. It was a revolving door of men. I spent all my free time on Grindr and a few other X-rated sites, seeing who was around and horny. This was a very experimental treehouse. I was a sexual deviant there. Sometimes, I would turn all the lights off and have a total stranger over. I wouldn't even see him, it was totally pitch black.

I had one regular guy who I was pretty into while it lasted. He was fit and hot. We met up at mine regularly as he worked near my place. He was bisexual and hadn't really hooked up with guys before. It's safe to say that I took the relevant initi-ation rituals very seriously indeed. I'd say we hooked up about seven times before it ended with me ghosting him because of a seriously serious run-in.

I was at work, sitting at a desk in the busy front reception area of the radio station, but kind of hidden from the sight of the pesky general public. I heard someone come in and tell the receptionist he was here to pick up tickets. The tickets were for the arena show *Walking with Dinosaurs*, well renowned as an amazing experience for the family. He proceeded to tell the receptionist that he was going to take his wife and kids. I craned my neck to see who this doting father was and got the shock of my life when I saw him. It was my bi-guy! The guy I had been fooling around with for weeks! I immediately dropped to the floor and hid under the desk. He didn't see me. We never spoke again. I still feel horrible about it.

After churning through most of the Newcastle population I moved to Adelaide, where I had a fresh start. I was going to be a respectable gay and not whore myself around like I'd done in Newcastle. I had matured into a proper adult and my slutty days were behind me. That lasted three hours.

Adelaide had a different breed of gay. Lots of closeted shy guys who I helped come out of the closet or, in one cruel case, retreat back into it. One guy who I invited over showed up, fired up and immediately afterwards was brutally honest and told me that he now knew for sure that he was definitely straight and thanked me as he left. So flattering. Glad I could be of use, M8!

Nowadays, I have a whole new set of issues to manage when it comes to my use of Grindr. With more than a million followers on various social media platforms, people tend to recognise you. So that makes being on Grindr rather difficult. I get a lot of messages from very attractive guys saying, 'Hi, I love your videos.' While that might sound like a dream come true, it's actually a bit of a headfuck. Most of them just want to say hi, however, I am there for one reason and one reason only. My profile name is 'FUN'—I don't know how much clearer I can be. Sometimes it can be confusing trying to figure out what people who message me want from me. Do they want fun, or do they just want to say hi? For me, Grindr is a place strictly for sexy times, so I have to be careful to not become a totally gross creep and drool over these guys when all they want is to be friendly from a distance.

The worst is getting a message from someone who shares my core whore values. The conversation gets steamy and nudes are exchanged . . . and then they drop, 'Are you that guy from Facebook?' Nothing scares me more. It totally derails the conversation and I don't know what to say. I usually say yes and just hope to god that they continue with the sexy talk.

I haven't quite integrated my public YouTube and Facebook persona with my private Grindr one. This might come as a shock, because I am very open about myself and my sexcapades on my videos and in my podcast, but it is a whole other thing when you're trying to be relatively anonymous on a hook-up app and the person messaging you already feels like they know you.

I'm no prize-winning beauty and I am totally aware of that, so I have had to come to terms with people on Grindr seeing my nudes and the reality that they might show them to other people. I would hope to god they don't, but I have to be realistic and understand that it might happen. As much as I am concerned for my privacy, I decided not to leave Grindr—after all, I need a reason to keep on living, don't I? Instead, I only send nudes that I am totally fine with. I have to love them.

I use nudes like candy, designed to lure men in. It doesn't work every time—my success rate on the app is like one in a hundred. But one per cent of the time, it works every time.

I often tell myself that it's just because I am busy—and I often am—but I no longer get anywhere near the amount of sexy times that I was getting in my Newcastle days. That's what happens when you let yourself go and Uber Eats enters your life as your significant other. And I'm definitely not a sex addict anymore. Sex is a punish and it's rare that I actually enjoy it. I mean, why get someone else over to play when you could just roll over and do it yourself.

18

A HEAVY SUBJECT

My weight. Man, has this been something that has haunted me most of my adult life. I don't understand my desire to be thin and I'm pretty sure that if I did ever get there, it wouldn't give me that euphoric feeling I'm so desperately craving.

Why does thin equal happy in my head? Why do I think all my problems will be solved by thinness? Where did it start and what caused this need to be skinny?

In my childhood, I was an average-sized kid weight-wise and Mum and Dad always made us eat healthily. We were super spoilt with a wide range of food choices and everything was great. I was always the shortest kid at primary school, but I was constantly told that I would hit puberty and grow. I don't remember the shadow of being fat lurking in the background for me when I was a kid the way it does now. It was a non-issue.

I think it was when I hit adolescence that everything changed. As I have said, I didn't have the best time in high school and, as a result, I became more isolated and a little closed off from the world. I liked to keep to myself and do my own thing.

Could this have been the start of the foodie journey and my cheese addiction? Everyone has hobbies—mine just happened to be eating and remaining still.

Another adolescence highlight was that I never did get that promised growth spurt. I'm five-foot-six as a thirty-three-year-old and I am totally fine with it. I did grow—but out, not up. I ate like a teenager, but I just didn't grow like one. I was a horrifically awkward-looking teen. I looked like a chubby lesbian and, truth be told, if I shave my beard I still do. This is why I have facial hair.

Throughout high school, I knew I was getting bigger but it was nothing to be concerned about—it was just a few kilos. It wasn't until I left school, got my licence and had the freedom to eat anything I wanted that things got totally out of hand. DRIVE THRU! That's the reason for my rapid weight gain. That exquisite combination of my sheer laziness and delicious fast food.

I didn't even have to get out of my car for a full meal. I'm sort of proud of the following story, but also a little bit ashamed. I was working full-time in retail and by the time the end of the day (finally) arrived, I would be starving. I still lived with Mum and Dad but on the way home, I would swing through Macca's Drive Thru and get a large Big Mac meal and two cheeseburgers. I would then eat them while driving home and finish the entire meal in the four-minute drive. I had a manual car too. That's impressive, I know, but also dangerous. I would do this almost daily.

I would then get home about six-fifteen and Mum would be making dinner. I would walk in the door, get changed and I would hear her call—and my Siren song—'Dinner's ready!' I would then run to the table and devour the meal she had prepared. WHAT A TOTAL PIG!

I was a beast. I could have been a competitive eater if I really stuck to it.

After retail, when I started working in radio, things went further downhill and fast. Radio is hard fucking work—it's the hours mostly, they really fuck up your system and routine. I'm not a morning person, so there were some days I would have to get up at four-thirty am and I wouldn't eat until eleven am. Then I would go home and sleep until the evening, at which point I would wake up and just eat whatever was in the fridge. It was never consistent meals, no thoughtful meal prep, and I actually had a fucked-up mindset that if I ate two unhealthy meals a day, that was like eating three healthy meals. Just genius logic.

My family have always been super supportive of me and have raised the odd flag here and there about my weight and health, but I would always feed them some bull-shit story about how I'm now woke to food and I got this, just you watch, I joined a gym, so now the weight will pour off me. Turns out you needed to go to the gym, not just join it, for that to happen. At one stage, I had two gym member-ships and a subscription to *Men's Health* magazine. I thought that's all I needed to do to be thin. I just don't want to have to do the work.

There was one time I put myself on diet pills. They prom-ised to blast the fat away. I bought them without reading any of the warnings or instructions. Turns out with any diet product, they only work in conjunction with exercising regu-larly and eating a balanced diet.

WHAT THE FUCK IS THE POINT?

Exercise and eating healthily are the annoying keys to weight loss. I bought these products to *avoid* eating healthily and exercising, but for these products to work you need to eat healthily and exercise? THAT'S BULLSHIT! These products are crap, but I totally bought into them. I JUST WANTED A MIRACLE PRODUCT THAT MEANT I COULD STILL EAT CHEESE BUT ALSO BE THIN.

I took those diet pills and didn't tell anyone. A week went by, and it felt like my appendix was about to burst. The pain in my stomach area was so sharp and so horrific I couldn't bend over or move without feeling like someone was stabbing me in the gut.

I was freaking out. I thought I was going to die, so I rushed myself off to the doctor. After some exams, he concluded the pain wasn't coming from my appendix so he ordered an ultrasound. The pain was so bad. I couldn't move, sitting to drive was horrible and I was convinced I needed my intestines removed. But when the ultrasound results came back in, they showed absolutely nothing.

My doctor was getting concerned and was contemplating big scary things. He asked me a series of questions about going on any new medicines. I told him I wasn't on any medicine, but I was taking diet pills. You should have seen his face. He looked like he was about to murder me. He told me I had just wasted my money and time and to stop taking the pills and to get out of his office. He was so furious.

It turns out that the pills had been causing the cramps and literally the next day I was totally fine. That was $750 well spent.

I only wish that was the only time I got myself into trouble medically while trying to lose weight.

Yet another quest to lose weight without changing my diet started when I stumbled across 'slimming tea' in an Asian grocery store. I bought it and proceeded to have a cup each morning with an unhealthy breakfast. It was guaranteed to help me shed the kilos and fast.

Two days into the tea routine, I was at work when my body started to make funny noises. My gut sounded like there was a heavy metal band in there performing at Coachella.

Then I needed a toilet ASAP. I had heard of people needing to poop, but I had never experienced this extreme need. I'd always been able to hold on until a bathroom was available, but this pain was extreme and I could feel my body forcibly trying to remove this excrement. I had never run so fast in my life. I dashed to the men's bathrooms and it was like NASA launching a rocket into space.

First, I thought I must have had food poisoning, and that now that the bad food had been expelled everything would be okay. I went back to my desk and comforted myself from the concerning experience with a nice hot cup of green tea, the slimming green tea. I felt better.

Ten minutes went by and another band joined the Gutchella stage, and this time they were louder and more aggressive. Again, I ran to the toilet and the SpaceX launch took off, with a LOT of fanfare.

I just sat there, convinced that I had just shat out my actual stomach and that I was about to die. After ten minutes on the toilet in the recovery position, I made my way back to my desk and everything was okay after that.

This went on for about five days. I thought there was something seriously wrong with me, but I was too scared to face it. I had almost just accepted my fate of dying alone, on the can, with a putrid expulsion my parting gift to the world.

It was day five and again I was sitting at my desk. I pulled out the green box of slimming tea and was making myself a cup in the office kitchenette when my friend walked in and spotted what I was doing.

'That stuff is potent,' she said and proceeded to tell me about her horrific toilet experiences while on the tea.

I gawked at her and instantly confessed to my own toilet near-death experiences. I said I had assumed I was seriously ill. She told me to read the back of the box. There, underneath a large warning 'If pregnant do not take', was the word: LAXATIVE. I was taking the world's most powerful laxative. I'm such a fucking moron.

I did lose two kilograms, but my anus has never recovered.

I then moved on to Weight Watchers, where I lost eight kilograms and, with a job change, quickly gained ten kilograms back.

Then I signed up to a program called Ultimate You where you eat nothing but leaves and do a spin class twice a day. I lost eight kilograms in six weeks and went on to drop a further four kilograms in the months that followed. I got down to eighty-three kilograms. I looked great but was not able to maintain it because I changed jobs again and my routine was disrupted.

I put it all back on.

My weight has yo-yoed for the last fifteen years and I have struggled to be comfortable with myself. I go through waves of loving myself and waves of loathing myself. Most of the time, I'm just uncomfortable and hate how I look, but all the positive comments I get from people make me feel better.

I'm lucky because that's not what's it like for ninety-nine per cent of my friends who are online. Mostly these friends are women and they are held up to the most ridiculous and horrible beauty standards. I don't know how they cope with faceless profiles being so utterly rude, commenting the most vile things.

I'm at a stage now where I know exactly what I need to do to lose weight. It's hard, it's really, really hard. I'm doing Jenny Craig, which has really assisted me as I don't cook and, so far, I'm on the right path. But given my track record, I'm doubtful.

I don't drink, I don't do drugs and I don't party. What I do is eat and eat and eat and I love it. It's fun and tasty and makes me happy.

19

CONSCIOUSLY UNCOUPLED

I get asked all the time not just about my sex life, but about my love life. People want to know if I have anyone special— and the answer is always a loud 'NO!' Not because I haven't found anyone, but because I don't *want* to find anyone. I think I am one of those people who just wants to be a spinster his whole life. I live alone and I'll die alone. That's what I want.

I'm often told that this will all change when I 'meet the right person', but unless I meet Zac Efron and we fall madly in love, then it ain't happening. I just have no interest in a relationship.

My take on relationships is pretty fucking simple: 'Sex with one person only and a lifetime of compromises.'

What is so appealing about that? I have sex with whoever I want and never have to compromise. Christian, what do you want for dinner? Christian, what would you like to do today? Christian, please feel free to leave the dishes in the sink and do them whenever. Why would I want this to ever change? I love my single life so unbelievably much.

I understand you might think that this makes me a selfish dickhead who puts his needs first and you are absolutely correct. I hate other people's needs. I live alone in a two-bedroom apartment with no responsibilities. I can't tell you how great it is. No pets and a few plants that thrive on neglect.

When I was younger, I mistook being horny for wanting to be in love. If I saw someone hot, I wanted to be with them, in a relationship. Then when I finally lost my virginity and became a whore, I realised that all I really wanted was a casual fling and then to be left the fuck alone.

I just like being alone. I want to be alone. Sure, I might have a stroke one day and my brain will change its mind, but after eleven years of not wanting a relationship in the slightest, I can guarantee you that I want to remain alone.

I learned a valuable lesson recently about projected happiness. This is a term I have made up—I'm not sure if it's something official, but it's where you project your idea of happiness onto someone else. I came to learn about this because I was the selfish one, projecting my idea of happiness onto someone else.

A good mate of mine was in a relationship that in my eyes wasn't working—it just didn't seem fun. The circumstances around it all were not great and I just couldn't understand how he was happy. He would call me and he would just mention stuff that would upset me quite a bit. I knew that if I'd been in the same situation, I wouldn't have been able to cope and I felt so bad for him.

I was starting to feel sad and I wanted out for him. But I only wanted him to leave because it would make me feel happy. I would feel this huge relief for myself. The moment I realised that I was being selfish was when I asked him if he was happy. He said he was and that he really wanted this relationship to work. All the shit he was going through, and he still really wanted it to work.

I came to the realisation that it's okay to have a different view on life and that the best thing to do is be there and be supportive. As soon as I came to that conclusion, I was okay.

The relationship I want is not the relationship other people want for me. They tell me that I'll want someone to be with, to travel with. What I have come to understand is that they are projecting what happiness looks like for them onto me. In a way, they pity me and think I'm unhappy because I'm alone. That couldn't be further from the truth.

My joy comes from the silence of home. The freedom to create whatever I want without someone there to stifle or question it. I have always done my best work alone and rarely collaborate with people.

My relationship really is with my career, if you can even call it that. I socialise and interact with my audience. I am inundated with messages and ideas and when everything gets too much, I can retreat to my place and be alone.

HOW MUCH MORE CONVINCING DO YOU NEED?!

I was asked by my editor to say more in this chapter. She said: 'This chapter's a little short: can you fill it with more detail? If you are not looking for love and a partner, what are you looking for in the future?'

Why do I have to be looking for something? Everything I have done in life has been on an impulse! I have never actively been looking for anything. Suddenly, it just happens.

I just upped and went to America without any planning.

I never planned to become a digital producer: someone got fired and I filled a void.

I didn't plan to make it big on social media: I just made a nurse video and then it happened.

I never planned to do a comedy tour: my management just booked it for me.

I got a message to appear in a movie: I didn't plan to ever be in a film. I certainly didn't plan for just the back of my head to be in a movie. Who would plan that?

I bought a car on a whim when I walked past a dealership, no thought went into it (BALLER MOVE!).

In 2020, I decided to move to Brisbane and bought an apartment up here all within the space of a month.

I opened a shop because there was a space available and I thought it's now or never. This wasn't something that was a goal or I had planned.

Nothing I have done has ever been planned or thought out. The only thing I was looking for and planning for was a successful radio career as a breakfast show host and that didn't happen. So, why plan?

I don't have any career goals. Where do I want to be in five years? Right here, doing what I am doing. It's fun. It led me to all these unplanned opportunities. Starring in a movie, being able to publish a book, doing a TV show (with Lou).

If I had a partner, I would need to plan things. I couldn't just make big decisions on my own—there would be someone else to think about. I don't want that. It stresses me out. I like doing things alone. It's purely a selfish thing. I have no desire for this to change. Life's good. I have my plants.

EPILOGUE

I want to finish this book with a letter to each of my parents. Can I ask that the font size be increased for this section, as they find it hard to see due to their age.

Dear Mum (Dad, I'll get to you in a minute),

You literally are the best mum in the world. I appreciate you. You did so much for me. From the gourmet lunches I got every day at school to having to drive me to band practice every Wednesday night. I remember everything.

I also want to tell you that you are the single worst driver I have ever seen ever. Like, actually so bad it is funny. You know we tease you about this but, Mum, it's true.

Do you remember that time we were driving through the Blue Mountains? High up on a clifftop and you were behind the wheel. I'm talking narrow winding road and you were paying no attention to the road. You kept screaming about how amazing the view was while the rest of us wet ourselves from the 800 near-death experiences we had around every corner.

There is nothing you can't do, and you always found time for everything and everyone. Running the school fete, designing the school uniforms, designing logos for the school band and organising and throwing the best birthdays. (If it were up to Dad, you know it would have been a frozen Mars Bar with a candle in it followed by us sitting around and listening to John Denver and then Dad going to bed at eight pm.)

You opened our home to family members who had fallen on tough times and took them in and cared for them. Your devotion to Nan was beyond anything I have ever seen. You visited her so often and I think your relationship with her was a pretty awesome one.

You are such a devoted mother and when the unthinkable time comes, I know I won't be able to handle it. You and Dad are my world and I cannot imagine it without you. Please for the love of god come back as a bird and check in on me once in a while.

I LOVE YOU.

Your favourite son,
Christian

•

Dear Dad,

I love you too.
    Send money.

Christian

JOKES!!!!!!

Dear Dad,

You have always been and forever will be my personal ATM. Even now that I am in my thirties, you still get out your wallet and without even asking will pay if we go out for dinner or when you and Mum visit and we go shopping—you always offer to pay.

You aren't just a walking ATM to me—you are also a walking gift shop. I remember when you would come home from your trips to America and we all helped you take your luggage upstairs. I want to say we were excited to see you, but we were more excited to see what gifts you had brought us. You never failed to deliver.

To be fair, we were always so excited to see you come home. We knew exactly when it would be and we waited outside for the taxi to drop you off. It wasn't the best when you went away on trips, but we knew why you had to do it (for some peace and quiet from the house of hell).

I also remember all the things you did for us. You built us our massive desks that took up the entire length of our walls—at the time, I didn't fully appreciate the size of those things: those desks were amazing, they could fit a computer from 1998 on them and still leave enough room to actually study (which I never did, but the thought was there).

Building the 700 extensions on the house so we could each have our own bedroom. The big backyard you maintained with Mum, the three gazebos you built and the fact you sold your hot air balloon to pay for a pool for us.

And you gave up the garage, the only space you called your own. For the last fifteen years, it has been filled with everyone's shit and you are unable to lock yourself away and do man things because it's actually full of actual shit.

Also, you are the butt of every joke we have ever made. We tease and belittle your eccentricities but secretly we love them. You always carry a Leatherman pocketknife everywhere, even to the airport. Why, Dad? It's a huge knife—why did you think that was a smart idea? What's funny is that we tease you, and then when something goes wrong we scream for you because we know you are the most prepared human on the planet.

I also need to mention that you are always contactable wherever you are. Your phone is attached to your hip, next to the Leatherman, and for that all four of us are eternally grateful. Mum is so useless with her phone, and if we need help we know you are always there.

There is so much to thank you for, but I want to close with this. You once cupped your hands when Nick needed to throw up on the plane on the way to Fiji and that was the most fatherly thing I have ever seen you do. He did throw up in them and you held that vomit for the entire landing and then waited for all the passengers to get off the plane before calmly walking into the toilet and cleaning yourself up.

You are an amazing father and when the times come to say goodbye, I will be so devastated if you haven't left everything to me in the will.

I LOVE YOU.

Christian (your favourite son)
P.S. Seriously, send money.

FOR THE FANS

I have a Facebook supporters page. This is about 1000 wonderful people who pay $4 a month to be a part of the 'Hull Family'. I offer them a few little extra things, one of which was to ask me some questions, which I would publish answers to in my book. I wanted an X-rated question, a meaningful one and a stupid one.

So, here I hand over to my fans. If anything in this section is stupid, offensive or boring, it is their fault and not mine. But I am excited to be able to include some of my fan interaction here, as my fans really are the most important part of everything I do and they are the secret to my success.

From the bottom of my heart, I thank them and owe everything to them.

FAN: JESSICA ELIZABETH

X-rated: What is the strangest thing that's turned you on?
Lesbian porn! I have watched some extreme woman-on-woman porn and it turned me on. I would love to go into detail, but the publishers don't really think that's a great idea. I was shocked at how fascinated and aroused I was by it.

Meaningful: What's been the most difficult/most rewarding part about taking a risk and leaving your job to follow a dream?
It's been so rewarding to be able to be my own boss, call the shots and do what I want to do. I think the fact I have got myself to this point is amazing and I'm so grateful. The difficulty is that there isn't any pressure—there's no direction and I have to come up with it all myself. What a dumb problem to have.

When you have a full-time job, you have KPIs, you report to a manager and you have a goal. When it's just you, suddenly that's all gone. It lacks structure and you have to figure everything out yourself—including what you want your next step to be. It's not always clear what the future holds or what your next move should be. Sometimes that's hard.

I also sometimes worry about pigeonholing myself as the dumb idiot comedian who collects Minis and eats chocolate (something I absolutely do, but don't want to be just that). I spent nine years learning about talking to an audience when I worked in the radio industry and five of those years working out how to do it online. In the future, I would like to share that knowledge—you know, teach and continue to grow and explore the online world and how it works, that kind of thing.

At this stage, I'm trying to create classes and tutorials people can take to help them better understand communities online. I'm suddenly really passionate about that and want to try that avenue. It's hard because people tend to see me as a lucky idiot who made it big because of a nurse video. But I have a tiny little bit more to offer, just a tiny, tiny fraction more.

I also love touring and doing live shows. I am keen to build a profile as a stand-up comedian, but that's years in the making.

I guess it is figuring all of that out that's the hardest part for me. And it is a job that's never finished—there is always a 'What next?' to be thinking about.

Stupid: What would you rather as a gift: unlimited Caramilk, Coles Minis forever or a Caramilk Coles Mini?

One hundred per cent, a Caramilk Mini! Please, make this happen, Coles!

FAN: AMY AFFLICTION (IF REAL, WHAT A GREAT NAME)

Meaningful: Who was your biggest inspiration as a child/teen to be comfortable to come out to your family?

I get this question all the time and I don't have an honest answer. That could be because I grew up in such a loving home, I didn't need to grasp on to anyone as a role model for me.

I honestly thought I was in a phase, and then by the time I was about thirteen or fourteen I realised I was gay. It just happened—I knew it was a thing, but I didn't personally know anyone else who was. I was never really terrified by it though.

My first real inspiration came later in life. Kyle Sandilands was who I wanted to be and comedy group Aunty Donna inspire me all the time with their hilarious humour.

X-rated: Do you prefer being the tunnel or the train?
Ha ha! I wish I could be the tunnel. The thought of just lying there putting in minimal effort is my dream. But being the tunnel is so painful so I'll occasionally be the train, but I have to be in the mood because being the train requires you to be a little bit fit which I am not.

FAN: DANNYEL HODGSKISS

Super stupid: Would you marry a woman, just cause?
No, I don't even think I would marry a man. I don't have any inclination to be in a relationship at this stage of my life and I don't think that will change.

Meaningful: Who is the person in your family you most look up to/idolise?
What a question! All of my family inspire me every day. My aunt Susie, Mum's younger sister, inspires me a lot. I don't

think she realises how much of an inspiration she is. She is unbelievably creative and wild and crazy. She does all this stuff and complains about it and she is basically me.

Her artistic ability is far beyond anything I can comprehend. I adore everything she creates. She is an amazing potter and sculptor, and she makes the most incredible mosaics and cooks the most amazing food. She is also such a massive fan of mine and always has been. Her support is so wonderful and has really made me feel like I am Beyoncé, of the family anyway.

But I could say that about all the members of my family. They are all so wonderful and supportive. I am so lucky that I don't have to take a shot of vodka to deal with my family. I love Christmases with them all and think they are all legends.

X-rated: Would you ever have sex completely naked in public?
You assume I haven't!

FAN: JOSEPHINE MALTESE

X-rated: Tell us the story of your first time!
My first time was so hot. It was with an older guy. I was twenty-three and he was about thirty-three. He was an insanely hot Lebanese guy. Tall, fit, hairy. I went over to his place, not thinking anything much was going to happen, but one thing led to another and then suddenly . . . oh, he is inside me! When I was younger, I was okay with foreign objects in me, but these days it doesn't agree with me.

Meaningful: If you could have dinner with anyone dead or alive, who would it be and why?

I think I would have dinner with my grandparents. Get to know them now that I'm an adult. We would talk about politics, their lives, and I'd share with them what's been happening with me. I'd love to know what they think. I'd also love to have dinner with my uncle one last time. He sadly passed away from prostate cancer.

FAN: KAREN EDWARDS

Meaningful: What advice would you give to someone questioning their sexuality?

If you are having a sexual crisis, it's absolutely normal. Everyone is so different. There are not boxes we go into, we can be fluid and our sexuality can change. When it comes to sexuality, we tend to think that we are locking ourselves into a life that we can never change or get out of. I know people who have been married with kids and then suddenly they realise they are gay. They still love and adore their family, but it's just not meant to be anymore. It's surprisingly not all that uncommon.

I think a lot of people confuse lust for love. If you lust for someone, it's not love—it's a need to explore your sexual side and then off you go. You never need to see them again.

It took me a few years to work out the difference. Every time I lusted after someone, I would confuse these feelings with being in love. I wasn't in love—I was just horny and wanted to get them naked. After hooking up with randoms for a few years, I realised that I was never in love with any of these boys. I just wanted them for their bodies.

So, I don't have advice, I don't know what you should do, everyone has a different life experience and there isn't an easy answer.

Stupid: What's your favourite flavour in ice cream, sorbet or gelato? Blood orange sorbet. Yummmm.

FAN: JESS MAC

Meaningful: You were fortunate to grow up in a home that was very welcoming of your sexual orientation and there are lots who won't and don't have that. You are also fortunate to be on a platform that allows you to really make a difference to the minds and hearts of those who are just like you. What message or advice do you have for the future generation? How can you help them and what can you say to help feel like they matter and also what advice can you give them in terms of not feeling ashamed of who they are? I'm so fortunate. I was lucky to come home to a welcoming family. School was another story, but my safe place was home. If this hadn't been the case, I would have felt extremely isolated and driven myself into a depression. I honestly don't know how some kids deal with the pressures of their parents, school and society all at the same time.

I think social media is an important tool for kids. It's a place they can realise they are important, they aren't alone and there are many kids in the same boat as them. For some kids, it can be a lifeline.

I think of it like this: you have grown up in a rural area and your community is small and very close. Everyone knows everyone and you literally can't be yourself for fear that you will be abandoned. You feel alone and you wonder what is wrong with you. You discover Instagram and your eyes are opened to the world. You see all walks of life being embraced and that's the moment you know you're not alone. This connection to the world is amazing, exciting and motivating.

The ability to connect with people across the world has made life easier in some ways and harder in other ways, but ultimately what these kids are able to get from an online community is support and love. Something that could be lacking in their home life. It's also a way to express themselves. Sure, TikTok is stupid to some adults but it's an amazing platform for kids to create and discover who they are.

What frustrates me the most in this situation is when parents refuse to understand the feelings their child has. I don't have kids and I don't know how hard and scary it would be to be a parent, but I do want to say this: if you have a child, no matter how old they are, if they have had the nerve to tell you they are gay and you have ignored them or told them they are wrong, you should be ashamed of your selfish behaviour.

FAN: JO MURPHY

Stupid: Would you rather fight a horse-sized duck or one hundred duck-sized horses?
Well, I'm deathly afraid of horses, so I'd take the horse-sized duck.

Meaningful: What did you envision happening when you started writing the book?
I started writing this book in 2017 as a way to cope with some external things going on in my life. It was a way to switch off from everything else that was happening and write about a life I am truly grateful for. I dreamed of having it published, but when I started it I honestly thought that was just a dream.

This book has made me reflect on my life and my journey and I'm so proud and thankful for all the people in my life. I'm probably going to lose my shit when I see it in a bookstore for the first time and by the time you are reading this I have no doubt done a thousand Insta stories trying to flog the book to as many people as I can. If you are reading this, then it means it has worked and you have bought the book. Unless you are just flicking through it at the bookstore with no intention of buying it, in which case I say to you: EITHER BUY ME RIGHT NOW OR PUT ME DOWN IMMEDIATELY!

I think the fact that I didn't have any expectations going into this book has made it what it is. It's not a forced word count, it's not rushed but most of all, it's something that I know my English teachers from school would be shocked by—that the person with the worst spelling and grammar has a book published.

X-rated: What is your most memorable Grindr hook-up?
There are so many and you want me to list just one! The most memorable was when a guy popped over on his way to work. I was living in Newcastle and was about twenty-six. HE WAS A FIREMAN! He came over in uniform and was totally ripped. It was like he just stepped off a calendar photo shoot. I died when I opened the door.

FAN: **BECK JOY**

X-rated: Spit or swallow?
I'll be shocked if this makes the final cut, but [redacted].

Meaningful: If you could go back in time, what advice would you give your sixteen-year-old self?
'Christian, just accept the fact that Dad is buying you a champagne-coloured Volvo to be your first car and be grateful for it.'

Stupid: Caramilk or KitKat Gold?
Both at the same time.

FAN: **MELANIE KING**

X-rated: If you don't like anal, how/when do you have that conversation with a prospective partner?

HAHA! I love that I'm so open about everything that people already know that my butt is an exit-only hole. I tell them straight up. You have to be honest when hooking up. That's why sometimes a high-angled pic can work against you—it may look good, but when your date comes over they will be able to see the real you.

Stupid: Do you take back everything you said about Caramilk when it was first discontinued and you said KitKat Gold was better? Truthfully, which is actually better?
That's like asking which gender is harder to raise: girls or boys. Both.

FAN: MEGAN WELLS

Stupid: Would you rather spend $10 buying something or spend $67 on craft items to make it?
I used to be obsessed with crafts and making things. When I lived with my parents, I was constantly creating. I loved it so much.

I once entered a submission for one of my favourite exhibitions, Sculpture by the Sea. I was going to make a huge fish net that would dangle off the cliffs at Tamarama on the east coast of Sydney. The fish net was going to be made of little wire fish all linked together. I thought it was such an awesome idea but sadly I didn't make it through.

As I got older, I realised the time involved in craft and the art I loved making and I just couldn't be fucked anymore. However, with lockdown and my move to Brisbane, I have gone full swing back into art-making and I am loving it. Now that I don't have a full-time job (as such), I can really involve myself in making things and I have opened a little retail shop to sell my wares. There is also the matter of the 'Fuck Off' flower pendants that I have been making consistently for the last few months. I have sold over 12,000 and the orders are not slowing down! So it's been a success.

Meaningful: Can you recall one moment that was your 'aha moment' and you knew you were on the exact right path at that time?
Never. My path has been an unexpected one. Never knowing what was ahead. I have little forks in the road and I have to choose. Some of those forks have a path going up a hill and a path that continues flat. I then have to decide whether I want to head up that hill or continue on a nice easy flat path. Most of the time, I choose the flat option—hills are hard, I don't want hills. I like my comfortable life.

My manager is always trying to get me to go up the hills. He is so good at pushing me to do things I would never do. He is the reason I chose the hill that led me to doing live shows and I'm so glad I walked up it. I hated it at first, but now it's so much fun.

But I've never had an actual 'aha moment'. The closest I've come to knowing that the path ahead was the right one was leaving full-time work to pursue the solo dream. I knew it was what I wanted to do and I could see that path for a few hundred metres ahead.

FAN: SARAH-JAYNE WILLOW

X-rated: What's the biggest dick you've ever sucked and can you deep throat?

Another question I will be surprised if the publishers let me leave in. I once had a guy come over and reveal literally a third arm in his pants. It was massive. It was like trying to put a fist in your mouth.

On the topic of deep throating, I will say I have had a lot of dick in my mouth, so much so that I have no gag reflex anymore.

FAN: SCOTTY PINFIELD

X-rated: Do you prefer cut or uncut? Giving or received head? What is your biggest turn-off that you come across most often?

Any pole's a goal! No real preference, I'll take anything. I'm turned off by biting and when guys get a little aggressive. Please don't slap me.

Stupid: What is on your bucket list?

I started writing this book in 2017, including this Q&A section. Therefore, my original answer to this question is now completely out of date. WHICH IS SO FUCKING EXCITING! Here is how I answered your question in 2017, Scotty:

> The thing I want most is to own my own home. For me, owning a home will make me feel so accomplished. It's so hard to get that in Australia. Property is so expensive and half of the apartments now are falling down. For some reason, I think I will be really proud of myself if I can buy a home without needing financial help from a partner. Don't get me wrong, I have had plenty of help getting to my goal. People signing up to become Facebook Supporters and pledging $4 a month, monetising my videos; if I do get there, it will be the house my fans built.

It's now 2020 and I managed to save enough to get a deposit and purchase an apartment in Brisbane. It's been the most rewarding thing to be able to do on my own. I never thought this day would come. I honestly thought I would be renting forever. I am now living the dream in the house my fans built. Thank you.

Meaningful: What makes you the happiest?
A clean and tidy house makes me really happy, however, I am so messy this almost never happens.

Meaningful: What is your biggest regret?
Yes, I have regrets. However, if I changed those regrets and never made those decisions, I wouldn't have learned the life lessons they taught me.

FAN: **MISTY MILLER**

X-rated: How many of your brothers' mates have you slept with?
Have I got a story for you! It was totally unintentional, but so funny. I was living at home still and my brother Tim had returned from a band camp thing in Hawaii. We all had to raise money for his school band to go over and perform in this big international concert. Mum, being a designer, had done the logo for the band and got all these T-shirts printed for all the students. It was a fabulous design.

A few months go by, and by then it was school holidays. I was on Grindr chatting with this guy. He was home alone and nearby, so I made my way over to his house. We had exchanged nudes and pics and very explicit messages, so it was about to go down. I arrive at his house and he opens the door and he is wearing the T-shirt that Mum had designed for the band's trip. I was a little shocked that I was about to hook up with a friend of my brother's, but it was also a little hot.

Just to clarify: yes, he had left school and was eighteen, and I was twenty-three. My brother laughed when I told him.

The other situation I got myself into was a little more awkward. I was chatting to this guy on Grindr and he was super discreet and wouldn't show me his face, but happily showed me everything else. He was, as they say, 'exploring his sexuality', so I ducked over to his place to help him 'discover himself'.

When I got there, he was naked and sitting on a chair in his living room. I instantly recognised him. He was a good friend of my brothers for years when they were younger and even played in their soccer team for a while. I WAS IN SHOCK! Literally, he was the last person I thought would want a dick in their mouth.

I did what I always do in those situations and respected his privacy. So, I raced home to tell my brothers. They were also shocked.

I have wanted to hook up with heaps of my brothers' friends (Matt C), but I think it would be super awkward, also they don't have many gay friends.

Wow, this makes me sound like a creep. I am a creep— why hide that fact!

FAN: TIFFANY ZANETIC

X-rated: What situation has made you just go 'Nope, no way, I'm not doing that!'?

I was once asked to shit in someone's mouth. That's such an aggressive sentence. I think I draw the line at that. I'm willing to explore my kinks, but blood and shit are out for me. I can't believe that was a question that someone asked. Point blank. 'Hey, hot pics, would you shit in my mouth?'

How does one's sex life get to that point? Well, I've done everything else and I'm bored now so it's on to eating shit! I shouldn't judge, everyone has the right to explore themselves. I feel like my life is heading in that direction haha. At sixty, I'm just messaging people to come over and shit on me.

Stupid: What big conspiracy in the world has you most unsure about what the truth is?

I'm obsessed with conspiracies. I watch so many documentaries and Shane Dawson videos. There are so many where I'm fifty-fifty. Here are my thoughts:

FLAT EARTH: Totally legit the Earth is one hundred per cent flat!

MOON LANDING: faked!

WATER: the government is controlling us via the water!

I'm joking. These are clearly not true, but I still watch videos about them. I love watching people's theories and seeing them trying to convince you that the Earth is flat. It's honestly mind-blowing.

One I don't want to believe but just seems so bizarre is 9/11. I know deep down it wasn't an inside job, but there are so many questions. I also believe the truth will always come out and to hide a secret that big is an impossibility.

In this day and age, it's too hard to fake or keep anything a secret.

FAN: **SARAH SPICER**

Meaningful: Was being gay easy for you to accept and deal with?

So easy. I'm surprised how easily I accepted it. I remember just thinking to myself, 'Oh, this isn't a phase, I'm gay.'

I had been teased in primary school and called a girl, but I never connected this to my sexuality. I was very gay as a kid hence why I was called a girl, but it didn't bother me at all. I didn't think being called a girl was an insult.

In high school, I was often asked if I was gay. This was a little confronting because I pretended I wasn't when, clearly, I was. I was never ashamed of it, I never wanted to change the fact I was gay—I just didn't want to open a can of worms for people to bully me more.

As soon as I left high school, I came out.

I love when young kids are themselves in school. It's inspiring. I could never do it. I was scared of what might happen.

ACKNOWLEDGEMENTS

If it wasn't obvious enough, my parents and brothers are mostly to blame for this book.

However, there are people not directly mentioned who I do want to give a shout out to. In particular, Holly and Jenny, my sisters-in-law. Why you chose to marry my brothers I'll never know but it's so great to have you officially in the family. You have always been so supportive.

I got a call from Holly recently—she gave me a big congratulations on finishing the book and told me she couldn't wait to read the parts about her. I told her there were heaps in the original draft, but sometimes the publishers need to edit bits and remove parts . . .

That same day I got an email asking if I wanted to write an 'Acknowledgements'. FUCKING THANK GOD! I'll put a bit about Holly in here. Jenny isn't as needy.

ACKNOWLEDGEMENTS

Dear Holly, please see above text. You're welcome.

A huge thank you to my editor Emma Rafferty who worked her magic on this book. When I wrote this it was a chaotic disaster, but she got out her red pen and sorted out the mess and built it into this amazing manuscript. Thank you Emma, I can't tell you how much you saved everything. Also a massive shout out to the ever-tolerant Tessa Feggans. She dealt with me pushing back deadlines and constantly asking for things.

I also want to thank Mrs Ciampa and Mrs Sawtell, two teachers who got me through high school. And Mr West, one of my teachers in primary school. He was very good looking.

In all seriousness, thank you to all of my friends and family for being so supportive of me and the things I do.

I asked Trish if she wanted to say anything and she asked me to include the following:

'Fuck off, I have no one to thank. I hate my kids and I just want a moment's peace—why should I have to write anything for this dumb book?'

PSST!

If you couldn't get enough of *Leave Me Alone*, you're in for a treat! Scan the QR code below for access to exclusive, behind-the-scenes content from Christian.